967 0833

CONGRESS
VERSUS
THE SUPREME COURT

1957–1960

Da Capo Press Reprints in

AMERICAN CONSTITUTIONAL AND LEGAL HISTORY

GENERAL EDITOR: LEONARD W. LEVY
Claremont Graduate School

By C. Herman Pritchett

CONGRESS

VERSUS

THE SUPREME COURT,

1957–1960

DA CAPO PRESS · NEW YORK · 1973

Library of Congress Cataloging in Publication Data

Pritchett, Charles Herman, 1907-
Congress versus the Supreme Court, 1957-1960.

(Da Capo Press reprints in American constitutional
and legal history)
Bibliography: p.
1. United States. Supreme Court. 2. Legislative
power—United States. 3. Judicial power—United
States. 4. United States—Politics and government—
1953-1961. I. Title.
KF8748.P69   1973   347'.73'26   73-249
ISBN 0-306-70568-0

This Da Capo Press edition of
Congress Versus the Supreme Court, 1957-1960,
is an unabridged republication of the first edition
published in Minneapolis in 1961. It is reprinted by special arrangement
with the University of Minnesota Press.

Published by Da Capo Press, Inc.
A Subsidiary of Plenum Publishing Corporation
227 West 17th Street, New York, New York 10011

CONGRESS VERSUS THE SUPREME COURT

C. Herman Pritchett

CONGRESS
VERSUS
THE SUPREME COURT

1957–1960

University of Minnesota Press MINNEAPOLIS

To Erna

IN MEMORY

PREFACE

THIS volume deals with the efforts in the 85th and 86th Congresses to "curb" the Supreme Court. The ostensible occasion for this effort was the series of decisions handed down by the Court between 1955 and 1958 in which it limited in one fashion or another official efforts to protect the internal security of the United States against subversion, on the ground that the programs were not authorized by legislation or were in violation of basic constitutional principles. In the minds of many members of Congress, this drive on the Court was also motivated by opposition to the 1954 ruling of the Court that racial segregation in the public schools was unconstitutional. The joinder of these two sources of antagonism to the Court resulted in a determined effort in Congress, not only to reverse certain decisions, but also fundamentally to limit the Court's powers of judicial review.

The failure of this effort at Court-curbing is full of significance for an understanding of the place of the Supreme Court in the American governmental system, as this volume attempts to make clear. The Court is at once a representative and a non-representative institution, an instrument both of politics and of justice. It is appropriate, and even necessary, that Congress should concern itself with the Court's decisions, but legislative interest must be expressed in a way which will not damage the essential values of the judicial institution. Judicial participation in democratic policy formation is an

American experiment which has to prove its worth to each new generation. The system operates through a complicated set of self-denying ordinances, both on the legislative and the judicial side, which can easily get out of order. The occasional crises that occur are not wholly without value if they renew our understanding of the rules by which we seek to achieve freedom with justice.

This study is an expansion of the Guy Stanton Ford Lectures I gave at the University of Minnesota in April, 1959. I wish to express my gratitude to the members of the University of Minnesota faculty who made the occasion of these lectures such a pleasant one, and particularly Professors Lloyd M. Short and Harold W. Chase of the Department of Political Science, and Dean William B. Lockhart of the Law School. Preparation of these materials was assisted by my appointment as Ford Research Professor of Public Affairs at the University of Chicago for the year 1958–59. Mr. Seyom Brown assisted in the preparation of the bibliography.

C. HERMAN PRITCHETT

CONTENTS

CONGRESS VERSUS THE SUPREME COURT

1

ЛЛЛЛЛЛЛЛЛЛЛЛЛЛЛЛЛЛЛЛЛЛЛЛ

CONGRESS
AND THE COURT

JUNE 17, 1957, was one of the memorable decision days in the history of the United States Supreme Court. At a time of great national concern over the threat of Communist subversion to American security and institutions, the Court handed down three decisions upholding the constitutional rights of communists or persons involved in official investigations of alleged subversive activities. In *Yates* v. *United States* the Court by a six to one vote found major defects in the Smith Act conviction of fourteen members of the Communist Party, ordering the acquittal of five and new trials for the remaining nine. In *Watkins* v. *United States* the Court by a vote of six to one held that congressional investigatory powers were limited by the provisions of the First Amendment and that questions asked must meet the test of pertinency to legitimate legislative powers. In *Sweezy* v. *New Hampshire* the Court by a vote of six to two appeared to recognize academic freedom as a constitutional right and imposed certain procedural limitations on the conduct of state legislative investigations.

These decisions were all the more remarkable because the Court had declined to exhibit much concern over comparable questions in earlier decisions. In *Dennis* v. *United States* (1951) the Court, with only two dissents, had upheld the constitutionality of the Smith Act in broad language and had refused even to look at the issues which in 1957 it found to be fatal to the convictions. During the years when Senator McCarthy and the House Committee on Un-American Activities were shockingly abusing congressional powers of investigation, the Court had avoided deciding any cases in which it might have had to face up to these issues.

This is not to say, of course, that the Court executed a complete reversal of direction on June 17, 1957, or that there was no basis in its earlier history for anticipating this concern for the safeguarding of constitutional rights. Three years earlier, the Court, with a few changes in personnel, had in the most portentous judicial ruling of the twentieth century unanimously declared that racial segregation in the public schools was unconstitutional.[1] This was the Court which had ruled in *Pennsylvania* v. *Nelson* (1956) that the federal Smith Act precluded the states from prosecuting sedition against the United States. This same Court had said in *Jencks* v. *United States* (1957) that a defendant in a criminal case was entitled to inspect reports to the FBI made by persons used as government witnesses and touching on events and activities concerning which they testified at the trial. This Court had reversed the action of New Mexico and California in denying admission to the bar to a former communist and to a man who had refused to discuss his political beliefs with the bar examiners.[2] Other decisions of similar import had been handed down by the Court prior to the June 17 decision day.

It would also be a misconception not to recognize that there were limitations in the *Yates*, *Watkins*, and *Sweezy* decisions which rendered their doctrine somewhat less sweeping than might have appeared at first glance. The *Yates* ruling did not question the constitutionality of the Smith Act, and left the government free to bring further prosecutions if it would abide by appropriate standards of evidence and proof. In both the *Watkins* and *Sweezy* decisions close analysis revealed that the actual holdings were somewhat more limited than was indicated in the rather bold language of the Chief Justice. Such considerations, however, did not minimize the tre-

---

[1] *Brown* v. *Board of Education* (1954).
[2] *Konigsberg* v. *State Bar of California* (1957); *Schware* v. *Board of Bar Examiners of New Mexico* (1957).

4

mendous impact of these three decisions on the country or detract from the symbolization they supplied of a judicial body ready and willing to defend the constitutional rights of even the most unpopular persons, and against the greatest pressures.

The decisions of 1957 aroused antagonism against the Court in many influential sectors of American opinion. The Supreme Court had of course been the object of extraordinarily violent attacks ever since the 1954 segregation decision, but organization of any reprisals against the Court would have required the acquiescence of a majority in Congress, which was clearly not obtainable on that issue. In fact, Congress had shown at least some disposition to promote the libertarian goals which the Court had espoused in the racial field by passing the Civil Rights Act of 1957, the first legislation for such a purpose adopted by Congress since the Reconstruction era. But the decisions of June 17, 1957, coming as they did on top of *Nelson*, *Jencks*, and other rulings upholding the rights of persons charged with subversive activities, led to attacks on the Court in Congress which were not limited by any regional lines.

It is not unusual for the Court to be criticized for decisions it has made. The American system of government has developed in such a way as to place responsibilities upon the Court which inevitably make it the subject of controversy, and bring it into conflict with the other two branches of the government. Nothing less than a history of the Court would be sufficient to demonstrate this fact, but perhaps a brief review of the controversies in which the Court has figured will provide useful perspective.

Previous Legislative-Judicial Disagreements

The Court's first major involvement with Congress occurred in 1793. The cause was the decision in *Chisholm v. Georgia*, where the Court ruled that a state could be sued in the federal courts by a citizen of another state. This was a clear misreading of the intent of the Constitution, and Congress, representing the irate states, quickly initiated the Eleventh Amendment to nullify the effect of the decision.

The Court almost as quickly got itself involved in partisan political

5

skirmishes. President Washington's appointees were uniformly Federalists, and often active in politics. John Jay during his tenure as the first Chief Justice spent one year in England on a diplomatic mission for the President, and ran twice for governor of New York. Samuel Chase, appointed in 1795, was blatant in giving effect to his Federalist views from the bench, and in 1800 a term of the Court could not be held because he was absent electioneering for Adams.

With the triumph of the Jeffersonians in the election of 1800, the Federalists sought to preserve something of their position by a retreat into the judiciary. John Marshall was appointed Chief Justice one month before Jefferson took office, and the Judiciary Act of 1801 created a number of new judgeships which were likewise filled with Federalists. The congressional Jeffersonians, once in power, could do nothing about Marshall, but they did undertake to impeach Justice Chase, though he finally escaped conviction. They also repealed the Judiciary Act of 1801, thus abolishing the posts of the newly appointed Federalist judges. When suit was brought to test the constitutionality of such legislative ouster, Congress shut the Supreme Court down by postponing its next term for fourteen months, by which time the controversy had died away.[3] But when the Court did meet in 1803 after its enforced vacation, Chief Justice Marshall used another controversy, the famous case of *Marbury* v. *Madison*, as the occasion for lecturing President Jefferson and asserting for the first time the Court's power to declare an act of Congress unconstitutional.

This degree of involvement of the Supreme Court in controversial issues of constitutional meaning and political alignment during the first decade of national life has been fairly typical of its subsequent history. There have of course been relatively quiescent periods. Another act of Congress was not declared unconstitutional until 1857, when the Missouri Compromise of 1820 was voided in the notorious *Dred Scott* decision. This ruling, which may have helped to make the Civil War inevitable, plunged the Court's reputation to its lowest depths. Congress undertook to juggle the size of the postwar Court for political purposes. When the Court showed signs of declaring

[3] See *Stuart* v. *Laird* (1803).

6

some of the Reconstruction legislation unconstitutional in 1868, Congress brusquely withdrew the Court's jurisdiction to decide the case.[4] Nor was the Court's prestige heightened by its antics on the legal tender issue where it first declared unconstitutional by a vote of four to three the legal tender acts under which the Civil War had been financed, and then within a year, after President Grant had appointed two new justices, reversed itself and upheld the acts by a vote of five to four.[5]

Another post–Civil War problem of greater magnitude for the Court was the interpretation and application of the Fourteenth Amendment. This addition to the Constitution had been drafted by a Congress dominated by Republican reconstructionists bent on using national authority to protect the newly freed Negroes from discrimination at the hands of the southern states. The Court, somewhat less sympathetic toward these goals, feared that use of the amendment's rather vague but all-encompassing language for these purposes would result in a fundamental readjustment of the balance of national-state power, and so it proceeded to draw most of the teeth from the amendment by casuistic interpretation.[6] This betrayal of congressional intent occasioned little or no congressional retaliation, for Congress had within a decade lost its postwar fervor for civil rights, and was willing to acquiesce in the erosion of the Fourteenth Amendment's standards for the protection of Negroes.

The new interest to which Congress turned in the latter years of the century was regulation of monopolistic industry and the concentrations of great wealth. Again the Court succeeded in frustrating this drive by eviscerating the Interstate Commerce Act and the Sherman Act, and by declaring the federal income tax unconstitutional.[7] This time, however, the Court collided with a powerful and continuing political interest, and Congress fought back. The Hepburn Act of 1906 and the Mann-Elkins Act of 1910 sought to undo the damage the Court had done to effective railroad regulation, and

---

[4] See *Ex parte McCardle* (1868).
[5] *Hepburn* v. *Griswold* (1870); *Legal Tender Cases* (1871).
[6] *Slaughterhouse Cases* (1873); *Civil Rights Cases* (1883).
[7] *United States* v. *E. C. Knight Co.* (1895); *Pollock* v. *Farmers' Loan and Trust Co.* (1895).

7

the Clayton and Federal Trade Commission Acts of 1914 endeavored to provide a firmer basis for the government's anti-trust efforts. The income tax decision was of course overridden by the adoption of the Sixteenth Amendment in 1913.

Nonetheless, the Court remained somewhat more conservative than Congress or the country, an attitude which was manifested in antagonism toward both state economic regulation and congressional legislation. At the state level there was, for example, the 1905 decision in *Lochner* v. *New York* invalidating a state ten-hour law for bakers. At the federal level there were at least two important illustrations. The federal child labor act ran afoul of a five to four Court decision in the famous case of *Hammer* v. *Dagenhart* (1918), and a minimum wage law for women in the District of Columbia was likewise declared unconstitutional in *Adkins* v. *Children's Hospital* (1923). Resentment from liberal quarters in Congress produced various retaliatory proposals. There were suggestions that the Constitution be made easier to amend, or that seven votes rather than a bare majority of the Court be required to declare an act of Congress unconstitutional, but these proposals came to nothing. The reputation of the Court as the ultimate guardian of property rights was confirmed both among its friends and its foes.

The New Deal and the Court

It was not until 1935 and 1936 that the Court came to a definite parting of the ways with the dominant opinion trends of the country as it declared several important New Deal statutes unconstitutional. The experimental legislation of the Roosevelt era took a year or two to work itself onto the Supreme Court's docket in test cases. The Court at that time contained two rather definite blocs – the liberal group of Brandeis, Stone, and Cardozo, opposed by the conservative McReynolds, Van Devanter, Butler, and Sutherland. The balance of power rested with the two remaining members, Chief Justice Charles Evans Hughes and Justice Owen J. Roberts.

Some initial tests in 1934 seemed to suggest that the Court would accept the new legislative trends by a vote of five to four, but this estimate soon proved mistaken. In 1935 and 1936 the Court invalidated a series of important federal and state regulatory laws, usually by a vote of five to four or six to three, depending upon whether Roberts alone, or both Roberts and Hughes, voted with the conservative bloc. The reaction against these defeats for the New Deal was organized by President Roosevelt, not by Congress. Following his electoral triumph in 1936 the President, who had had no Court vacancies to fill during his first term, undertook to eliminate the judicial barrier to reform by a proposal to increase the Court's size to fifteen justices. This "Court-packing" plan produced a struggle of great bitterness in Congress and the nation, and it was eventually defeated by Congress. Instead, Congress passed a liberalized retirement act to encourage the older justices to leave the bench, and within a short time resignations permitted President Roosevelt to make over the Court more nearly in his own liberal image by new appointments.

The Roosevelt Court was one of the most fascinating courts in American history.[8] The New Deal drive had largely spent its force in Congress by 1938, which was just when the Court began to feel the liberalizing effect of its new members. During the next decade or so the Court was for almost the first time in our national experience more liberal than Congress or the country. There was consequently no reason for the Court to exercise any restraining influence upon congressional use of regulatory powers, particularly the commerce power, which only a few years earlier had been the battleground between Court and Congress.

But soon new areas of tension began to build up around civil liberties problems. Initially these issues arose in the states: there were censorship cases, compulsory flag salutes in the public schools, attempts to limit press freedom, and failure to observe due process in criminal prosecutions. The Roosevelt Court dealt with such civil liberties issues in an unprecedented number of cases, endeavoring to develop a justification for judicial intervention in behalf of libertarian values by elaborating on the "clear and present danger" test first stated by Justice Holmes two decades earlier. The Court was by no means unanimous in its conception of its civil liberties

[8] See C. Herman Pritchett, *The Roosevelt Court* (1948).

role, however. Serious doctrinal differences developed over the degree of "activism" which the Court might appropriately manifest, but in a substantial number of cases a majority of the justices did accept the responsibility of striking down state or local action which infringed on First Amendment or due process values. For the most part congressional legislation was not involved in this flurry of civil liberties cases. By the time the Court got around to examining alleged congressional interference with freedom of speech by abusive use of the investigatory power, or the application of the federal Smith Act in the prosecution of communists, the judicial temper had been changed by President Truman's appointments. Chief Justice Vinson had replaced Harlan F. Stone on the latter's death in 1946, and Justices Frank Murphy and Wiley B. Rutledge, probably the two stoutest libertarians on the bench, had died in 1949. The Vinson Court was consequently much less concerned with the protection of libertarian values, and no clashes with Congress developed over such issues.[9]

The Warren Court

On Vinson's death in 1953, President Eisenhower appointed Earl Warren, governor of California, as Chief Justice. By 1957 he had added John M. Harlan, William J. Brennan, Jr., and Charles E. Whittaker to the Court.[10] It is one of the paradoxes of American history that President Eisenhower's appointees were largely responsible for swinging the Court's balance back toward a more liberal orientation. President Truman was a liberal and constantly at odds with Congress, yet the Court which was dominated by his appointees showed a diminished concern for civil liberties and a marked deference to Congress. Under President Eisenhower, a conservative who conscientiously sought to avoid clashes with Congress, the Court for a period took on a startlingly liberal tone and incurred congressional attacks sharper than any for almost a century. A campaign to reverse the Court's 1957 decisions and to limit its

[9] See C. Herman Pritchett, *Civil Liberties and the Vinson Court* (1954).

[10] Justice Whittaker did not participate in the *Yates, Watkins,* and *Sweezy* decisions.

powers to render such decisions in the future got under way immediately in Congress. One success was achieved very rapidly. Congress adopted on August 30 a measure accepting the general principle of the *Jencks* decision but providing for its application in a somewhat more restricted fashion than the Court had contemplated in its ruling.[11] No other results were achieved in the short time prior to the close of the session in 1957.

The drive was renewed in the 1958 session, as a bewildering variety of bills were presented to "curb the Court." That body, far from retreating in the face of this assault, counter-attacked on June 18, 1958, with *Kent* v. *Dulles*, in which by a five to four vote it ruled that Congress had not authorized the Secretary of State to deny passports to communists or suspected communists or to demand noncommunist affidavits from citizens applying for passports.

The drive against the Court in Congress reached its climax in the final week of the session, between August 19 and August 23. In spite of the fact that several of the anti-Court bills passed the House and that there was probably a Senate majority for some of the proposals, a determined effort by a group of Senate liberals, a ruling by Vice President Nixon, and some mistakes by the sponsors of the measures led to the adjournment of Congress without a single one of the proposals having been adopted.

All of the major Court-curbing bills were re-introduced when the 86th Congress convened in January, 1959, and the legislative mills once more began to grind, with the House again taking the lead. But before any legislation had reached passage stage, the Supreme Court had another momentous decision day. This time the date was June 8, 1959. In two decisions, *Barenblatt* v. *United States* and *Uphaus* v. *Wyman*, the Court by a narrow five to four margin upheld broad federal and state legislative investigatory power and in the process substantially modified and limited the supposed doctrines of the *Watkins*, *Sweezy,* and *Nelson* cases.

This result was achieved by a majority composed of one Roosevelt appointee, Felix Frankfurter; one Truman appointee, Tom Clark; and three Eisenhower choices — John M. Harlan, Charles E. Whit-

[11] S. 2377, Public Law 269, 85th Cong.

11

taker, and Potter Stewart, the latter a 1958 addition to the Court. The bitterly protesting minority was made up of the Chief Justice plus Justices Black, Douglas, and Brennan — two Eisenhower and two Roosevelt appointees. This was an alignment which had become increasingly familiar since 1957, but these two decisions were its most important manifestation. The four dissenters had all been part of the majority in the *Watkins*, *Sweezy*, and *Nelson* cases, the Chief Justice having written the opinion in all three.

Interpretations and explanations for the *Barenblatt* and *Uphaus* decisions varied widely. One theory frequently offered was that they constituted a strategic withdrawal from controversial positions under pressure of Congress and some sectors of public opinion. From this point of view the decisions would parallel the tactics of the "switch in time that saved nine" in 1937, when the Court made its peace with the New Deal by upholding the constitutionality of the Wagner Act. It is significant that Justice Harlan, writing the *Barenblatt* opinion, and Justice Clark, author of *Uphaus*, both went out of their way to reassure Congress that the Court understood the threat of communism and the need for legislative power to deal with it. Additional support for this theory is supplied by four decisions on June 22, 1959, in which by the same alignment the Court gave a most deferential interpretation to the statute Congress had passed in 1957 to limit the effect of the *Jencks* decision.[12]

A second explanation was that the Court had been shifted back toward a more conservative position by President Eisenhower's two most recent appointments, Whittaker and Stewart. Others contended that the division on the Court was not between liberals and conservatives in any meaningful usage of those terms, but instead grew out of the justices' attitudes respecting use of the Court's powers of judicial review. This division was commonly characterized as one between "activists" willing to use their judicial authority to achieve what they believed to be the goals and purposes of the Constitution, and advocates of self-restraint who were less disposed to controvert the legislative will.

[12] *Palermo* v. *United States, Rosenberg* v. *United States, Pittsburgh Plate* v. *United States*, and *Galax Mirror* v. *United States* (1959).

Finally, it was suggested by some that the decisions of June 8, 1959, were not in fact reversals of the actual holdings of the earlier cases, but only amounted to a clarification and explanation of the rather general language used there. Warren wrote the *Yates, Sweezy,* and *Nelson* decisions, and Brennan was the author of *Jencks*; in each instance the language employed was somewhat stronger than the actual holding of the Court. Probably Justices Harlan and Frankfurter, for example, had never really subscribed to the language of the Court's opinions in the earlier cases, and so could regard their positions in the two sets of cases as perfectly consistent.

Whatever the explanation for the 1959 decisions, the Court's change in direction had an immediate effect in reducing congressional enthusiasm for Court-curbing legislation. It is true that on June 24 the House passed a bill which had been drafted to void the *Nelson* holding, but the vote was much closer than it had been when the same bill passed the preceding year — 241 to 151 in 1958, and 225 to 192 in 1959. Other anti-Court legislation also passed the House. On July 7 the so-called Mallory bill was adopted by a vote of 262 to 138. This measure was intended to modify a 1957 Court ruling which had voided a conviction for rape in the District of Columbia on the ground that the suspect had not been arraigned and advised of his legal right to remain silent with sufficient promptitude after his arrest. Then on September 8 the House passed by a vote of 371 to 18 a moderate passport control measure, after beating back efforts to give the Secretary of State authority to rely on confidential informants in denying passports. None of these measures reached floor consideration in the Senate, however, and few anti-Court measures even emerged from Senate committees. Thus the 1959 session of Congress ended, as did that of 1958, with no anti-Court legislation. The 1960 session, dominated by the struggle to adopt a civil rights act giving increased protection to Negro voting, saw the drive for Court legislation practically forgotten.

So once again, as in 1937, the Supreme Court emerged from a test of strength with its great constitutional powers unimpaired. In 1937 it had achieved this result by abandoning the line of decisions which had brought it into conflict with the democratic forces of a

13

new world which the justices had not comprehended. In 1958 and 1959, however, there was no judicial retreat on the major issue of segregation. The Court held firmly to its insistence on perceptible, even though slow, progress toward the constitutional goal announced in 1954. But on some of the other issues which had aroused opposition in Congress, and particularly on the question of legislative investigatory powers, the Court majority did retreat from the bold position taken in 1957. For its victory the Court, just as in 1937, paid a price in the reversal of doctrine.

From a perspective of almost a quarter of a century, it is now generally agreed that the price paid by the Court in 1937 was the just and necessary consequence of judicial folly. In the current situation there is no such unanimity that the Court was well-advised in yielding a measure of its concern for the protection of individual freedoms against official pressures. In this controversy are involved basic issues concerning the nature of judicial responsibility in a democratic society which have recurred continuously throughout American history.[13] While those issues can never be finally resolved, they may be clarified by the following examination of the most recent controversy between Court and Congress.

[13] For a powerful statement of the case for judicial protection of fundamental freedoms, see Charles L. Black, Jr., *The People and the Court: Judicial Review in a Democracy* (1960).

14

2

工工工工工工工工工工工工工工工工工工工工工工工

THE MATERIALS OF
CONTROVERSY

THIS book is concerned primarily with the congressional reaction to the Supreme Court's decisions in certain national security cases, decided mostly in 1957 and 1958. However, it is necessary to bear in mind that the legislative temper was also affected during that period by decisions dealing with other problems, a factor which contributed substantially to the sharpness of the congressional reaction to the national security decisions.

The Segregation Issue

First of all, there was the bitter opposition that had developed, primarily in the South, against the Court's historic decision in the case of *Brown* v. *Board of Education* (1954). This declaration of the unconstitutionality of racial segregation in the public schools was a challenge to the customs and the way of life of an entire section of the country, and in spite of the gradualism authorized by the Court in moving toward the goal of racial integration in the schools, it was inevitable that resistance to compliance with the decision would be bitter, violent, and fed by the deepest well-springs of passion and emotion.

The Court in the *Brown* case had unanimously found that the rule of "separate but equal" was no longer an acceptable standard for judging the constitutionality of segregationist legislation or administrative practice. "Separate but equal" had been accepted by the Court in 1896 in the famous case of *Plessy* v. *Ferguson*, where it was used to justify a state law requiring segregation of the races on public transportation. The Supreme Court subsequently proceeded on the assumption that the same standard rendered segregation in public education constitutional.

In fact, of course, segregated educational facilities for Negroes were almost never "equal" to the white schools, and the Supreme Court eventually took note of this fact. In *Sweatt* v. *Painter* (1950) the Court held that a small and poorly staffed law school for Negroes, which Texas had set up in 1947, was not the constitutional equal of the University of Texas Law School. In 1952 the Court held hearings in five cases where the equality of segregated education at the primary and secondary school level had been challenged. After delays proportional to the gravity of the questions raised, the Court in 1954 was finally ready to hold that segregated facilities, even if equal, were an unconstitutional violation of the equal protection clause.

Having announced this conclusion, the Court allowed a full year to pass before issuing its plan of action for putting the decision into effect. The cases were remanded to the courts where they had originated, which were to fashion decrees of enforcement on equitable principles and with regard for "varied local school problems." Desegregation actions or proposals of the various school authorities would come before the local federal courts for determination as to whether they constituted "good faith implementation of the governing constitutional principles."

Numerous devices were developed by the legislatures and executives of most of the southern states to frustrate the Supreme Court's demand for action "with all deliberate speed," and suits affecting the desegregation issue were instituted in a number of the lower federal courts. For several years the Supreme Court declined to get involved in reviewing these decisions, but the problems at Little Rock, Arkansas, finally drew a Supreme Court ruling in September, 1958.

During the preceding fall, efforts to place in effect the judicially approved plan for desegregation in Little Rock had been maneuvered by the governor into a riotous situation which President Eisenhower was finally forced to control by calling in federal troops. The Little Rock schools were subsequently closed. In June, 1958, the federal district judge in Little Rock ordered a two and a half year delay in the integration program, but his order was reversed by the federal court of appeals in August. The Supreme Court, meeting in special session, unanimously affirmed the judgment of the appellate court on September 12 in the case of *Cooper* v. *Aaron*. The violent resistance to the school board's desegregation plan the preceding year was held to be "directly traceable" to the governor and state legislature of Arkansas, and the Court refused to permit the constitutional rights of Negro children to be sacrificed to the violence thus instigated by official state action.

The Court, moreover, took pains to make clear that any "evasive schemes" for continuing segregation, such as turning public schools over to private organizations for operation as "private schools" with some kind of state financial assistance, would not be acceptable. "State support of segregated schools through any arrangement, management, funds, or property cannot be squared with the Amendment's command that no State shall deny to any person within its jurisdiction the equal protection of the laws," the Court unanimously concluded.

Subsequently, in November, 1958, the Court did accept as constitutional a tactic which might delay, at least temporarily, the progress of desegregation. Pupil placement laws were generally adopted by the southern states after 1954, which authorized school boards to assign students to schools on such bases as nearness to schools, scholastic aptitude of the pupil, and wishes of the parents. Race was not stated in any of these statutes as a placement factor. A three-judge district court in Alabama assumed that the statute would be administered on a basis of individual merit without regard to race or color. "If not," the court added, "in some future proceeding it is possible that it may be declared unconstitutional in its applications." The Supreme Court affirmed this decision in *Shuttlesworth* v. *Birmingham Board of Education* on these "limited grounds," thus giving clear notice that any provable use of pupil placement statutes

17

to achieve racial discrimination would bring a declaration of unconstitutionality.

From 1954 onward the Supreme Court was subjected to constant attacks in Congress, principally by southern representatives, because of the segregation ruling. Often these assaults were vituperative in the extreme, calling into question not only the ability but also the motives and the patriotism of the justices. However, southern congressmen could expect only scattered support from their colleagues in other sections of the country on the direct merits of their segregationist stand. The southerners were therefore alert to the need to find a broader base for their opposition to the Court, on which they might be joined by other allies.

The States' Rights Issue

Invoking the rhetoric of the historic claims of states' rights was an obvious method of achieving this goal. This tactic was made feasible by the fact that decisions of the Warren Court in other areas had also had the effect of challenging state powers. The *Nelson* decision, though dealing specifically only with the effect of the federal Smith Act on state sedition statutes, was grounded on general propositions concerning the exclusion of state authority by federal "preemption" or "occupation of the field." Again, the Warren Court had ruled unfavorably to the states in a number of cases under the Taft-Hartley Act, thus providing additional fuel for a general attack on the Court's performance of its traditional role of umpire in federal-state relations.

There were, moreover, the resentments that had long been developing over the Court's enforcement of due process standards in state criminal prosecutions. The due process clause of the Fourteenth Amendment makes the Supreme Court the ultimate judge of the standards of procedure in criminal prosecutions throughout the country. The Court early held that the states are not bound by the specific procedural requirements of the Fourth through the Eighth Amendments, which apply only to the federal government.[1] As the

[1] See *Hurtado* v. *California* (1884); *Twining* v. *New Jersey* (1908).

18

Court said in *Snyder* v. *Massachusetts* (1934), a state "is free to regulate the procedure of its courts in accordance with its own conception of policy and fairness unless in so doing it offends some principle of justice so rooted in the traditions and conscience of our people as to be ranked as fundamental."

The fact that this standard is such a general one means that it can be interpreted with considerable flexibility. Since the 1930's the aspects of local criminal administration which have been most under Supreme Court scrutiny have been the provision of counsel, the use of force or coercion to secure confessions, racial discrimination in the selection of juries, and fairness of trial generally. On occasions the Court's decisions dealing with these subjects have been subjected to vigorous attack in the states, and contentions that the Court is handicapping state law enforcement by doctrinaire concern for the rights of criminal suspects have been heard.[2] Exercise of habeas corpus jurisdiction by the federal courts, which is the device by which federal review of state convictions is often achieved, has also come under congressional assault, and numerous proposals for limiting such jurisdiction have been considered in Congress.

The Court had thus affronted or thwarted a variety of localistic interests which could be expected to unite in resistance and reprisal. To these motivations the Court added by its national security decisions in 1956 and 1957 the potential opposition of all those organizations and individuals who regarded anti-communism as the primary obligation of national policy. The emotional intensity which can be generated by appeals to or manipulation of the widespread fear or hatred of communism was fully demonstrated by Senator McCarthy's success in the exploitation of these attitudes. The Warren Court laid itself open to attack from these quarters by decisions which had

[2] During the period under examination, the decision affecting criminal procedure which drew greatest fire in Congress was a case arising in the District of Columbia, *Mallory* v. *United States* (1957), and involving federal rather than state law. The conviction of Mallory, a Negro, for the rape of a white woman was unanimously reversed by the Supreme Court because after arrest he had not been arraigned without unnecessary delay, as required by law. Instead, he had first been subjected to intensive questioning by the police, who succeeded thereby in securing a confession from him. On this entire subject see C. Herman Pritchett, *The American Constitution* (1959), chap. 30.

19

the effect of protecting the rights of communists or persons suspected of being communists.

In the existing perilous world situation, many Americans and many powerful organizations of Americans believe that communists are not entitled to claim constitutional rights, or that the communist conspiracy is so dire a threat to the internal security of the United States that traditional freedoms must be suppressed in order to counter the greater evil of communist subversion. Under these conditions an effort by the Supreme Court to guarantee certain basic constitutional rights to persons whom the government sought to punish because of their alleged connection with the communist conspiracy naturally aroused a storm of opposition.

Thus it was because certain decisions of the Warren Court, in defending basic libertarian values, controverted strongly entrenched localistic interests and strongly held anti-communist views, that the attack on the Court burgeoned into one of such great proportions. Opponents of the segregation decision alone could not have achieved this result. Nor could the opposition to the Court based on its efforts to keep the anti-communist drive within the bounds of the Bill of Rights, standing alone, have achieved such success. It was the simultaneity of these affronts which resulted in the program of massive retaliation against the Court.

Pressures on the Court

In the government itself, the pressures on the Court came primarily from Congress, and they will be detailed in the following chapters. President Eisenhower took a generally neutral position. On the segregation issue, he consistently refused to express any opinion on the merits of the original decision in 1954, in spite of repeated urgings that he declare himself. His expressed position was that his oath of office required him to enforce whatever decisions the Supreme Court might make, and it was in pursuance of this duty that he sent the troops into Little Rock. As for the Court's national security decisions, he occasionally expressed some puzzlement as a layman about the judicial reasoning, and he never appeared to be much concerned about the Bill of Rights issues which worried the

Court. On the passport decision, he accepted the evaluation of the Department of Justice that an extremely serious situation had been created requiring immediate legislation by Congress to correct.

So far as the Department of Justice was concerned, under Attorney General Brownell it undertook little initiative or leadership in assisting with plans for enforcement of the segregation decision. But after the lesson of Little Rock, and under Attorney General William Rogers, the Department's attitude changed to one of active effort to develop a strategy of enforcement and to anticipate the problems and dangers that might develop. The Department of Justice expressed its opinion, sometimes favorably and sometimes unfavorably, on bills proposed in Congress to counter the Court's national security decisions. The most vigorous general defense of the Court to come out of the Department during this period was a strong speech by Solicitor General J. Lee Rankin in March, 1959, before an American Bar Association meeting in Pittsburgh.

Though our attention in this study is focused on Congress, it is obvious that congressional action and opinion were influenced by attitudes expressed by the press, the bar, and other organizations and pressure groups. While it is impossible here to take any general account of these various opinion sources, it is necessary to note two documents which, because of the respected character and presumed expert knowledge of the organizations which issued them, played an unusually important role in the deliberations of Congress and in the country generally.

On August 23, 1958, the Conference of Chief Justices of the states, meeting in California, approved a 30-page report of its Committee on Federal-State Relationships as Affected by Judicial Decisions (see pp. 141–159). This document indicted the Supreme Court's decisions as having seriously encroached on the position and constitutional powers of the states. For example, the report charged that "the overall tendency of decisions of the Supreme Court over the last 25 years or more has been to press the extension of federal power and to press it rapidly."

The Court had, the report went on, "too often . . . tended to adopt the role of policy-maker without proper judicial restraint."

21

The frequent differences of opinion among the justices and the occasional overrulings of prior decisions caused the authors of the report "grave concern as to whether the individual views of the members of the Court as from time to time constituted, or a majority thereof, as to what is wise or desirable do not unconsciously override a more dispassionate consideration of what is or is not constitutionally warranted."

The chief justices feared that the Supreme Court had grown impatient "with the slow workings of our federal system. That impatience may extend to an unwillingness to wait for Congress to make clear its intention to exercise the powers conferred upon it under the Constitution . . ." The report concluded:

It is our earnest hope which we respectfully express, that that great Court exercise to the full its power of judicial self-restraint by adhering firmly to its tremendous, strictly judicial powers and by eschewing, so far as possible, the exercise of essentially legislative powers when it is called upon to decide questions involving the validity of state action, whether it deems such action wise or unwise.

This resolution was adopted by a vote of 36 to 8. The chief justices of California, New Jersey, Pennsylvania, Rhode Island, Utah, Vermont, West Virginia, and Hawaii cast the negative votes. The chief justice of Pennsylvania, who had written the majority opinion in the *Nelson* case for the state supreme court, thought that "these strictures on the Supreme Court are entirely uncalled for and certainly are not justified on the basis of the decisions, which the report cites for criticism . . ." The chief justice of New Jersey said:

I question the wisdom, and indeed the propriety, of a joint pronouncement by this Conference of Chief Justices, assembled as it is in an official or quasi-official capacity. I doubt that it is within the proper function of this Conference to issue what is in essence a blast, devoid of any specific recommendation as to any specific matter. Most importantly, in my judgment, the criticism and characterizations in the Report are unwarranted.

The report was welcomed by all the opponents of the Court and heralded as expert confirmation of the criticisms which had been made in Congress and elsewhere. The report itself carefully avoided any criticism of, or indeed any reference to, the Court's segregation decisions, but certainly much of the feeling underlying the report had been generated by the segregation controversy, and the report was immediately seized on as a weapon to discredit the decision in *Brown* v. *Board of Education*. Governor Faubus of Arkansas, for example, began his address to the special session of the state legislature on August 26, 1958, with a quotation from the report.

A second significant set of recommendations for action affecting the Supreme Court appeared on February 24, 1959, when the House of Delegates of the American Bar Association adopted resolutions in Chicago urging that Congress pass legislation reversing the Supreme Court's interpretation in virtually every one of the decisions it had handed down in national security matters (see pp. 137–140). This is the language of the resolutions which is particularly relevant:

WHEREAS, recent decisions of the United States Supreme Court, in cases involving National and State security and with particular reference to Communist activities, have been severely criticized and deemed unsound by many responsible authorities; and

WHEREAS, problems of safeguarding National and State security have been exposed or created thereby which this Association feels would be best solved by the careful study of each decision, and the prompt enactment of sound amendments to existing laws within the Constitutional powers of the Congress;

NOW, therefore, be it resolved that this Association recommend to the Congress the prompt and careful consideration and study of recent decisions of the United States Supreme Court and the preparation and passage of separate amendments to the laws involved so as to remove any doubt as to the intent of the Congress, and to remedy any defect in the existing law revealed by the decisions.

The more specific recommendations of the resolutions will be discussed in detail later in this volume. The Bar Association's Special Committee on Communist Tactics, Strategy and Objectives, which drafted the resolutions, dismissed the concerns which the Court had expressed about Bill of Rights issues as "technicalities" which should not be permitted to stand in the way of the punitive action sought by the government. The report, moreover, did not seriously consider the possibility that constitutional issues might be involved if the statutory revisions proposed were made. Officials of the Bar Association subsequently denied that the report was intended to be a criticism of the Court, but that was of course the only possible interpretation of the adoption of the recommendations, and the document was of great influence in the campaign to curb the Court.

3

⊓⊔⊓⊔⊓⊔⊓⊔⊓⊔⊓⊔⊓⊔⊓⊔⊓⊔⊓⊔⊓⊔⊓⊔⊓⊔⊓⊔⊓

ATTACKING THE
JUDICIAL INSTITUTION

IN GENERAL there are two lines of strategy which Congress can employ when it undertakes to engage in controversy with the Supreme Court. One is to attack the decisions of the Court to which it objects. The other is to attack the Court as an institution.

Let us consider the first alternative. Where the objectionable decision is based on a judicial interpretation of a congressional statute, Congress can show its disapproval by amending the statute. If the Court has found that a statute means one thing and Congress intended it to mean something else, Congress can readily make its will prevail by writing its meaning specifically into the law. Subsequent chapters will examine the congressional campaigns to subject numerous decisions of the Warren Court to this type of legislative review.

Where the Court rests its ruling on an interpretation of the Constitution, however, Congress faces a much more difficult problem in "correcting" the Court's view. A constitutional amendment can be launched in Congress, but this is a long and involved process, and the odds against eventual success are almost prohibitive. It is when they are faced with this situation that opponents of the Court tend to move over to the other possible strategy and plan an attack on the Court itself — its status, its function, its prestige, its members. This chapter is concerned with the effort of Congress, primarily concentrated in the 1958 session, to mount a major assault aimed at weakening and penalizing the judicial institution.

Congressional Weapons

It is often inadequately realized that Congress can, merely by passing a statute, effect major changes in the status or powers of the Supreme Court. First, it can increase or reduce the number of members on the Court. As already noted, this tactic has been used or attempted several times in the past, the most recent being President Roosevelt's unsuccessful effort to pack the Court in 1937. The inglorious defeat suffered in that campaign has made it unlikely that this strategem will soon be repeated.

Second, Congress can undertake to specify qualifications for appointees to the Court.[1] No really concerted effort toward this goal has ever been made, but numerous bills were introduced in the 85th and 86th Congresses with such provisions. The contention of those who supported these efforts seemed to be that some of the justices appointed to the Court since 1937 were unqualified by training or temperament for judicial functions.

One common feature of these proposed measures was a requirement that appointees to the Court must have had prior judicial experience. President Eisenhower himself sponsored this notion in several public statements, and his choices for the Court subsequent to Chief Justice Warren were in fact all previously federal or state judges, at least for a short period. Most of the congressional bills insisting on this background agreed on five years of previous judicial service. Experience on a state court was accepted, some measures specifying that it must be on a state supreme court,[2] and others accepting any state court of general jurisdiction.[3] A variation of this plan required that one of every two Supreme Court appointees must have had ten years of judicial service at the time of appointment.[4]

[1] There may be some basis for argument that Congress cannot by statute limit the President's freedom of choice in appointing Supreme Court justices, but Congress has been proceeding on the assumption that it possesses such power.

[2] For example, H. R. 304, 85th Cong.

[3] See H. R. 421, 85th Cong.   [4] H. R. 658, H. R. 1200, 85th Cong.

A number of other qualifications were also suggested in these bills. In some instances these proposed restrictions seemed to be aimed at particular members of the Court. One bill proposed that members of Congress, heads of federal executive agencies, and governors of states, should be ineligible for appointment to the Court for a five-year period after leaving office.[5] This provision would have disqualified Justice Black, a senator at the time of appointment, Justice Douglas, a member of the Securities and Exchange Commission, Chief Justice Warren, governor of California, and Justice Clark, a former Attorney General. In other bills it was proposed that appointees must be natural-born citizens of the United States,[6] which would have disqualified Justice Frankfurter had it been in effect before his appointment.

A third kind of limitation on the Court which Congress may effect by statute is the withdrawal of certain types of cases from the Supreme Court's appellate jurisdiction. Such a withdrawal has actually been legislated by Congress on one occasion in American history,[7] and it is a most severe blow at the prestige of the Court. A proposal of this kind, known as the Jenner-Butler bill, was one of the key retaliatory measures introduced in Congress after the 1957 decisions; it will be discussed in more detail later.

Apart from these three major types of statutory retaliation, some rather more bizarre bills were introduced in Congress to give effect to legislative displeasure with the Court. The *Brown* decision, in which the Court reversed a precedent of some sixty years standing and cited certain social scientists to support its conclusions about the effect of racial segregation on schoolchildren, was undoubtedly the inspiration for the following proposal:

The courts of the United States and the courts of the several States of the United States shall not be bound by any decision of the Supreme Court of the United States which conflicts with the legal principle of adhering to prior decisions and which is based upon considerations other than legal.[8]

[5] H. R. 304, 85th Cong.
[6] H. R. 320, H. R. 2270, H. R. 2922, 85th Cong.
[7] *Ex parte McCardle* (1869).
[8] H. R. 10775, 85th Cong.

27

Then there was Senator Eastland's suggestion that newly appointed federal judges be required, in addition to the regular oath, to swear that they "will not knowingly participate in any decision to alter the Constitution."[9]

Should Congress wish to look beyond statutory modes of reprisal and utilize constitutional amendments as means for attacking the Court, other possibilities are opened up. Several proposals were put forward to strip Supreme Court justices of life tenure and make them subject to appointment for four year terms, with the possibility of reappointment.[10] Ten-year terms were also mentioned. Even more drastic was the 1958 proposal of Senator Long that the country be divided into nine judicial districts, from each of which a Supreme Court justice would be elected by the voters for an eight-year term, the judges so chosen to elect one of their number as Chief Justice.

Constitutional amendments have been proposed during various periods of American history to limit the Supreme Court's power to declare acts of Congress or state legislatures unconstitutional. During the 85th Congress there were several bills in Congress, stimulated by the segregation controversy, providing that the Supreme Court could invalidate a provision of a state constitution or statute only by unanimous decision of the justices participating. The sponsors apparently felt that this limitation could be accomplished simply by statute.[11] More cautiously, another congressman suggested a constitutional amendment to give Congress power, by a two-thirds vote, "to limit the authority of courts of the United States to determine that statutes of the United States or of any State are repugnant to the Constitution of the United States."[12]

Beyond statutes and constitutional amendments, there is always the impeachment process. Threats to institute impeachment proceedings against one or more of the justices were heard frequently in Congress during these years, and in 1957 the Georgia legislature voted to request the state's representatives in Congress to bring im-

[9] *New York Times*, April 2, 1958.
[10] See H. J. Res. 32, 85th Cong.
[11] H. R. 4565, H. R. 4659, 85th Cong.
[12] H. J. Res. 73, 85th Cong.

peachment charges against no less than six members of the Court. No serious attempts of this kind were actually instituted.

Recent appointees to the Court, however, have been subjected to intensive questioning by opponents of the Court's decisions when their names came up for confirmation in the Senate. In the case of three appointees — Warren, Brennan, and Stewart — the confirmation process was complicated by the fact that they had been given recess appointments, and so had served for a period on the Court before their confirmation hearings were held by the Senate.

Before the Eisenhower administration, no recess appointment had been made to the Supreme Court for over a hundred years. The last instance was the appointment of Benjamin Curtis in 1851. In the case of Eisenhower's three recess appointments, the vacancy in each instance had occurred while Congress was not in session, and the President's position was that the Court should not be left at less than full strength for any appreciable period of time. Not only would a vacancy increase the work load of the remaining justices, but the possibility of tie votes would be created.

These are considerations of some weight, but the perils of recess appointments are also considerable. Chief Justice Warren was confirmed before the Court became the subject of controversy, but both Brennan and Stewart found themselves in dangerously exposed positions by reason of their recess appointments. Justice Brennan took his seat on October 16, 1956, and was not confirmed until March 19, 1957. Justice Stewart began service on October 14, 1958, but did not achieve confirmation until May 5, 1959. Thus both men served the greater part of a term without assurance that they would win acceptance from the Senate. Litigants before the Court during those periods were partially denied the trial before life-tenure justices that the Constitution promises. The holders of recess appointments would certainly be more than human if they did not occasionally speculate on the effect which their decisions might have on the ultimate confirmation vote. It may well be questioned whether a justice, who must still run the gantlet of confirmation, can achieve complete independence from ulterior influences on his decisions, no matter how great his integrity.

Consideration should also be given to the consequences that would ensue should a recess appointee be refused confirmation, as actually happened in the case of Chief Justice John Rutledge in 1795. The decisions in which the rejected justice participated would stand under those circumstances, but their intellectual authority might well be affected, particularly if the unseated justice had cast a deciding vote.

During his confirmation hearings Justice Brennan was queried about his views on the powers of congressional investigating committees by Senator McCarthy who, while not a member of the Senate Judiciary Committee, was permitted to ask questions of the appointee. Brennan refused to answer some questions on the ground that they bore on cases pending before the Court.

Justice Stewart in his turn was asked whether he was a "creative judge," or one who would follow the precedents; whether the Constitution meant the same thing now that it did in 1787; and whether he agreed with the "reasoning" of the Supreme Court's decision on segregation in 1954. The members of the Judiciary Committee themselves disagreed on whether Stewart should answer this last question. Stewart took the position that an answer would not be appropriate, but he did say: "I would not like you to vote for me on the assumption or the proposition that I am dedicated to the cause of overturning that decision, because I am not." The Senate eventually confirmed Stewart by a vote of 70 to 17, but Senator Hart of Michigan stated during the debate that he thought the necessity of examining a sitting Supreme Court justice embarrassed both the nominee and the members of the Judiciary Committee, and he concluded that recess appointments hampered the Senate in performing its constitutional duty of confirmation.[13]

[13] *Congressional Record*, May 5, 1959, pp. 6708–9 (daily ed.). On August 29, 1960, the Senate adopted by vote of 48 to 37 the following resolution (S. Res. 334):

"Resolved, That it is the sense of the Senate that the making of recess appointments to the Supreme Court of the United States may not be wholly consistent with the best interests of the Supreme Court, the nominee who may be involved, the litigants before the Court, nor indeed the people of the United States, and that such appointments, therefore, should not be made except under unusual circumstances and for the purpose of preventing or ending a demonstrable breakdown in the administration of the Court's business."

The Legislative Proposals

The congressional attack on the judicial institution reached its climax during the 1958 session, which was the second session of the 85th Congress. The anti-Court forces were repulsed in the last week of that session without achieving a single one of the goals they had sought. An account of the handling of the Court problem during this period should be very helpful in indicating the nature of the defenses available to the Court against a legislative assault.

The most direct and serious attack on the Court as an institution was the bill introduced by Senator William E. Jenner of Indiana on July 26, 1957, about a month after the *Yates* and *Watkins* decisions. The bill sought to employ the power given Congress by the Constitution to regulate the appellate jurisdiction of the Supreme Court. According to Article III, section 2, the Court's appellate jurisdiction is to be exercised "with such exceptions, and under such regulations as the Congress may make." As already noted, Congress had previously used this authority once in the post–Civil War period to withdraw from the Court's jurisdiction a case on which argument had already been heard by the Court.

Senator Jenner selected five areas in which he disapproved of the Supreme Court's decisions, and his bill proposed to withdraw each area of controversy from the Court's appellate jurisdiction so that in the future such cases could not be decided by the Court.[14] His bill would have deprived the Court of appellate authority (1) over admissions to the practice of law in the state courts; (2) with respect to any function or practice of any congressional committee or subcommittee, the jurisdiction of any such committee, or any action or proceeding against a witness charged with contempt of Congress; (3) with respect to administration by the executive branch of its employee loyalty-security program; (4) over any statute or executive regulation of any state the general purpose of which is to control subversive activities within the state; and (5) with respect to rules, by-laws, and regulations of school boards or similar educational bodies concerning subversive activities among teachers.

[14] S. 2646, 85th Cong.

31

Hearings on this drastic measure were held for one day (August 7, 1957) by a subcommittee. It was then reported favorably to the full Senate Judiciary Committee, which referred it back to the subcommittee with instructions to hold more extensive hearings. This killed the measure so far as the first session of the 85th Congress was concerned. In the second session, hearings were held in February and March, 1958. On return of the bill to the full committee, extensive amendments were proposed by Senator Butler of Maryland, and as amended the bill was approved by the committee by a vote of 10 to 5 on April 30, 1958.

The Butler amendments substantially changed the character of the bill. Because of the widespread opposition which had been expressed against the device of limiting the Court's appellate jurisdiction, four of the subjects which the original Jenner bill had forbidden the Court to touch were dropped. Under section 1 of the revised bill only appellate jurisdiction over admission to the practice of law in state courts was to be denied to the Supreme Court. However, the Butler amendments then went on to add to the bill additional sections which sought to provide remedies of other kinds for the grievances with which the original bill had dealt.

Section 2 was a response to the *Watkins* decision. It empowered congressional committees to decide for themselves on the pertinency to the legislative purposes of the committee of questions asked, whenever this objection was raised by a witness. It also confirmed the power of a congressional committee to control its own investigations, subject to the will of its parent house.

Section 3 of the Jenner-Butler bill would have restored enforceability of the some 43 state anti-subversive statutes which had been knocked out by the *Nelson* decision. Section 4 was a rebuttal to the *Yates* decision, amending the Smith Act in three respects to make it applicable to the current activities of the Communist Party in the United States. While the Jenner-Butler bill was thus a substantially modified version of the original Jenner bill, it still retained in section 1 the basic challenge to judicial authority, control over the Court's appellate jurisdiction.

The other principal bills affecting the Court which came under

32

consideration in the 1958 session should be identified briefly. In most instances they will be discussed in more detail in the chapters which follow. The *Nelson* decision motivated several additional legislative proposals. The House passed H. R. 3, a drastic anti-Nelson bill, on July 17, 1958, by a vote of 241 to 151. This bill did not stop with restoration of the effectiveness of the state sedition laws rendered unenforceable by the *Nelson* ruling. It sought rather to state general principles to govern, and limit, all future Court decisions dealing with alleged conflict between federal and state laws. This same principle was also introduced in a Senate bill, S. 337, by Senator McClellan of Arkansas. The Department of Justice filed strong opposition to this measure, which it criticized as so broadly drawn that its future effect could not be foretold.

The Court's views on the federal loyalty-security system for government employees were at issue in several bills. The Court had decided three cases between 1955 and 1957 in this area — *Peters* v. *Hobby* (1955), *Cole* v. *Young* (1956), and *Service* v. *Dulles* (1957). In each case the Court had upheld the attack on the system, but always on rather narrow grounds which did not reach any constitutional issues. The decision with the most potential impact on the existing loyalty-security arrangements was the *Cole* case, in which the Court had held that the powers of summary suspension and removal on loyalty-security grounds extended only to employees in "sensitive" agencies, and that for non-sensitive agencies the regular dismissal procedures remained in effect. A bill was developed to overturn this decision, providing that all employees of any department or agency of the government were deemed to be employed in activities involving national security, and so subject to summary removal.[15]

The passport issue was injected in the midst of the 1958 session, when the Supreme Court decided the case of *Kent* v. *Dulles* on June 18. The State Department charged that this judicial challenge to the Department's statutory authority to refuse the issuance of passports had created a dangerous emergency requiring immediate congressional action, and forwarded to Congress a proposal for a sweeping

[15] S. 1411, 85th Cong.

33

grant of passport authority to the Department. On July 7 President Eisenhower sent a message to Congress in which he said: "I wish to emphasize the urgency of the legislation I have recommended. Each day and week that passes without it exposes us to great danger."

The House committee was willing to act, but recognized that the broad measure requested by the State Department could not be passed in the short time remaining of the session. Consequently a more restricted bill was developed.[16] It gave the Secretary of State authority

to deny a passport to any person who is a member of or former member of, or affiliated with, the Communist Party, or who knowingly engages or has engaged, since 1948, in activities intended to further the international Communist movement, as to whom it is determined that his or her activities or presence abroad would under the findings made . . . be harmful to the security of the United States.

The bill forbade the denial of an application for a passport without a hearing, and provided for judicial review of denials. This measure was reported out unanimously by the House committee, but in the Senate no committee action was taken.

In addition to these national security decisions, the Court was also under attack during the 1958 session because of its ruling in *Mallory* v. *United States* (1957). As already noted, in *Mallory* the Court had unanimously voided a District of Columbia conviction for rape on the ground that the defendant, a Negro, had not after arrest been brought without unnecessary delay before a committing officer for arraignment. Instead, he had been kept by police and questioned intensively until a confession was secured. The principal anti-Mallory bill, largely drafted by Representatives Keating of New York and Willis of Louisiana, provided that

(a) Evidence, including statements and confessions, otherwise admissible, shall not be otherwise inadmissible solely because of delay in taking an arrested person before a commissioner or other officer empowered to commit persons charged with offenses against the laws of the United States.[17]

[16] H. R. 13760, 85th Cong.
[17] H. R. 11477, 85th Cong.

34

This bill passed the House on July 2, 1958, by a vote of 294 to 79. In the Senate the Judiciary Committee reported it out with the addition of one word, "reasonable," inserted in front of "delay." The position of the Senate committee was that the original bill might positively encourage delay in arraignment on the part of federal law enforcement officers, by providing that delay, no matter how prolonged, could never be a ground for ruling confessions inadmissible.

The Last Week of the 85th Congress

Like a mystery play which brings all the murder suspects together in the same room for the third-act climax, all these legislative proposals of an anti-Court character reached a showdown in the Senate during the last week of the 85th Congress. The House had already made its decisions. It had passed four bills dealing with the Court — H. R. 3 (the broad preemption bill), the Mallory bill, the Cole bill, and a bill to limit federal judicial review of state criminal trials by habeas corpus. It still had under consideration the bill to restore the State Department's control over the issuance of passports.

The Senate had been much less impetuous. It had passed in 1957 the measure which the House subsequently turned into the Cole bill to extend the federal loyalty-security system to non-sensitive jobs.[18] But the other bills noted above were still before the Senate, and the passport bill was still in committee. The progress of these measures depended in large part upon the strategy which the Senate majority leader, Lyndon Johnson, chose to follow. The Senate was badly divided on most of these proposals, and Johnson was under strong pressure from both sides.

The Jenner-Butler omnibus bill was recognized as the most extreme proposal before the Senate and the most direct rebuke to the Court. Southern senators, led by Richard Russell of Georgia, pressed Senator Johnson to bring it up for a vote. Johnson refused, fearing that the bill would split the Democrats badly. He agreed instead to take up three of the other bills — the Nelson,[19] Mallory, and habeas

---

[18] S. 1411, 85th Cong.; as passed by the Senate this measure would have made the impact of the security system somewhat less harsh on its victims.
[19] S. 654, 85th Cong.

corpus measures. This strategy had very great advantages for him. All three of these bills were favored by the Eisenhower administration. Their passage would constitute a criticism of the Court which would please the southern senators. On the other hand, he hoped that the defenders of the Court would be placated by the pigeonholing of the Jenner-Butler bill. His plan also called for bringing up the three-bill package before the Senate considered the essential Mutual Security appropriation bill, so that extended debate on the Court measures would be prevented by the necessity of passing the foreign aid measure before adjournment. This was a sample of the parliamentary management which had earned Johnson a deserved reputation as perhaps the most skillful Senate leader in history.

However, the approaching end of the session meant that any determined group of senators bent on defending the Court could wreck these plans by prolonged debate. In fact, a group of about ten Democratic liberals, led by Hubert Humphrey and Paul Douglas, let Johnson know that they would fight the bills. This prospect led Johnson to temporize during the week of August 11. By the end of the week he had resolved that he must go ahead and give the opponents of the Court their opportunity. On Saturday, August 16, the Senate Democratic Policy Committee announced that the three bills were to be taken up for action before adjournment, which was scheduled for the following Saturday, August 23.

On Tuesday, August 19, Johnson called up the Mallory bill, with the Senate Judiciary Committee's "reasonable" amendment. The Senate liberals agreed that "reasonable" improved the bill, but even so they opposed it because of its recognized animus toward the Court. As Senator Javits, New York Republican, said:

Were I not convinced . . . that this is but the first bill dealing with dissatisfaction with decisions of the Supreme Court, and if I did not realize that the record made in connection with this measure will be a great indication to the country, as well as to our colleagues, of how we think about the entire problem raised by various decisions of the United States Supreme Court I would not make this presentation [against the bill] today.[20]

[20] *Congressional Record*, vol. 104, p. 18489.

Johnson had hoped that the bill would be disposed of quickly. Instead, the debate ran on all day and well into Tuesday night. An effort by the anti-Court forces to eliminate "reasonable" from the bill was narrowly defeated by a vote of 39 to 41. Another amendment, offered by Senator Ervin of North Carolina, sought to limit the effect of the *Mallory* decision by providing: "The trial judge shall determine from the surrounding circumstances whether the delay is reasonable, and his determination shall be binding upon appellate courts if it is supported by substantial evidence." [21] This amendment was snowed under, 18 to 62. But Senator Morse's attempt to get into the bill the principle that no arrest by a federal officer could be made without warning the person arrested of his right to remain silent was even more heavily defeated, 13 to 64. Finally the Mallory bill with "reasonable" retained was passed 65 to 12, the opposition consisting of eleven liberals and Senator Butler. [22]

The bitter day-long debate on this measure had ruined Johnson's hopes and plans for quick passage of the three-bill package. Neither side had accepted his compromise. The southerners now demanded the right to vote on the Jenner-Butler bill, and Johnson, knowing he had the votes to defeat it, acquiesced. On Wednesday he called up a non-controversial bill concerning federal appellate procedure in cases involving the orders of certain administrative agencies, [23] and then yielded to Senator Jenner to permit him to offer his bill as an amendment. Both Senators Jenner and Butler made long statements on behalf of the bill, [24] and there were relatively brief rebuttals by Senators Hennings of Missouri and Wiley of Wisconsin. Then Hennings' motion to lay the amendment on the table was adopted, 49 to 41. [25] Senator Johnson voted with the majority, while Senator Knowland, the Republican leader, was with the anti-Court minority.

Senator Douglas then sought to counter-attack by offering as an amendment to the bill a positive statement of support for the Supreme Court, in these words:

[21] *Ibid.*, p. 18512.
[22] *Ibid.*, p. 18520.
[23] H. R. 6789, 85th Cong.
[24] *Congressional Record*, vol. 104, pp. 18635–77.
[25] *Ibid.*, p. 18687.

The Congress hereby expresses its full support and approval of the recent, historic decisions of the Supreme Court of the United States holding racial segregation unlawful in public education and transportation as a denial of the constitutional right to the equal protection of the laws.[26]

Several senators rose to object that it was outside the constitutional powers of Congress to pass resolutions either approving or disapproving decisions of the Supreme Court. Senator Douglas replied:

I ask my colleagues, what have we been doing all afternoon? What has the Judiciary Committee been doing by passing on some of these questions? The . . . so-called Jenner-Butler bill, which was recently tabled, was a thinly apparent effort to overrule no less than five Supreme Court decisions. . . .

This is all part of a "reverse the Court" campaign which stems largely, although not entirely, from the earlier decision . . . in the Brown case. . . .

What our good friend is apparently contending for is that Congress has the right to disapprove the decisions of the Court, but does not have the right to declare its approval of the decisions of the Supreme Court. My friend is arguing that we must embark on a one-way street; that we should overrule the Court, but never support the Court.[27]

Senator Long, however, thought there was a clear difference between the two situations. When there is a disagreement with the Supreme Court's interpretation of a law, it is necessary to adopt legislation to revise that interpretation, and this is a proper legislative function. But where there is agreement with a judicial interpretation, a resolution stating that agreement can serve no purpose except to "glorify" the Court's decision. No vote was taken on the Douglas amendment, for Senator Johnson was able to substitute the Nelson bill as the pending order of business.

The Nelson bill was no sooner before the Senate than Senator McClellan arose to offer the broad preemption bill, H. R. 3, as a substitute for it. After some debate Senator Hennings moved to lay the McClellan substitute on the table, but his motion was rather

[26] *Ibid.*, p. 18688.
[27] *Ibid.*, p. 18693.

unexpectedly defeated by a vote of 39 to 46.[28] This development apparently took Senator Johnson by surprise, and since it was 11:30 at night he immediately secured adjournment, over the protest of the southern sponsors of H. R. 3.

The next day, Thursday, August 21, the battle resumed. Standing alone the Nelson bill would have been impossible to defeat, but the attaching of H. R. 3 to it had made it more vulnerable. Senator Carroll of Colorado moved to recommit the bill as amended to the Judiciary Committee, and Senator Johnson worked all day to secure the votes for recommittal. Late Thursday night the motion to recommit carried by a single vote, 41 to 40, and to all intents and purposes the 1958 assault on the Supreme Court had been defeated.[29]

There were some further developments, however. On Thursday, while the recommittal battle was taking place on the floor of the Senate, the conference committee which was dealing with the two different Cole bills that had passed the two houses agreed on a report. The House accepted the conference report the next day,[30] but it never got action in the Senate. Senator Olin Johnson, the chairman of the conferees, was reportedly not in favor of the bill, and had yielded to the House conferees only in return for other concessions by them. Senators Clark and Church had also opposed the bill in conference, and they were unreconciled. Senator Clark was apparently able to persuade Johnson not to bring the conference report before the Senate, and so this measure died also.

The House passed a passport bill on Saturday, August 23, the last day of the session,[31] but there had been no committee action on such a bill in the Senate. Consequently, the only measure left for Senate action on Saturday was the Mallory bill, which had gone to conference after its passage by the Senate on the preceding Tuesday, with Senator O'Mahoney as chairman of the conference committee. The House conferees had objected to the Senate specification that only confessions secured during periods of "reasonable" delay in arraign-

[28] *Ibid.*, p. 18748.
[29] *Ibid.*, p. 18928.
[30] *Ibid.*, pp. 19176–8.
[31] *Ibid.*, pp. 19653–9.

ment would be rendered admissible by the new legislation. The conferees had arrived at a compromise which retained "reasonable" but added a proviso: "That such delay is to be considered as an element in determining the voluntary or involuntary nature of such statements or confessions."

The relationship of this language to the original bill was somewhat confused. The *Mallory* decision had not been concerned with whether a confession was voluntary or involuntary. It held that *any* confession was invalid if secured during a period of delay in arraignment, and the original bill with its Senate amendment proposed to change this rule so that only unreasonable delay in arraignment would void a confession. Now the conference amendment sought to relate the factors of delay in arraignment to voluntariness of confessions. As Senator Wayne Morse put it, what had originally been an arraignment bill was now a confessions bill.

When the conference report reached the Senate floor early Sunday morning, Senator Carroll raised a point of order that the new language was not in either the House or Senate versions of the original bill. His contention was that the conferees had gone beyond the bounds of their assignment, which was to agree on either the House or Senate versions or something in between. Vice President Nixon, presiding during the last hours of the 85th Congress, sustained the point of order,[32] and the battle was over. The almost incredible result was that every legislative proposal directed against the Court's decisions had been defeated.

We now turn to examine in more detail the six principal issues raised by Supreme Court decisions on which Congress chose to do battle with the Court.

[32] *Ibid.*, p. 19576.

4

⊓⌐⊓⌐⊓⌐⊓⌐⊓⌐⊓⌐⊓⌐⊓⌐⊓⌐⊓⌐⊓⌐⊓⌐⊓⌐⊓⌐⊓⌐⊓

THE LEGISLATIVE
INVESTIGATION ISSUE

Watkins v. *United States* was one of the two decisions on June 17, 1957, which galvanized the Court's opponents in Congress into action. In the *Watkins* case the Court dared to criticize the operations of the House Committee on Un-American Activities, and to indicate an intention to assume some responsibility for determining whether congressional committees were operating within their constitutional authority.

Only once before in its history, in the 1881 decision of *Kilbourn* v. *Thompson*, had the Court undertaken to curb a congressional investigating committee, and a considerable body of opinion had developed to the effect that Congress was the final judge of its powers of investigation. Actually, such an idea could not be supported by judicial opinions. On the contrary, the Supreme Court had been clear from the beginning that if Congress turned over to the courts the responsibility for punishing as criminal alleged contempts of congressional authority, it would have to permit the courts to determine to their own satisfaction that contempt had occurred, and that Congress had been defied while exercising its legitimate authority.

Kilbourn v. *Thompson* held invalid a House investigation into a bankrupt firm, of which the United States government was one of the creditors. The Court pointed out that the matter was not one on which Congress could validly legislate. Moreover, the controversy was then pending in the courts, so that Congress was precluded from intervening by the principle of separation of powers. In 1927 *Mc-Grain* v. *Daugherty*, while upholding a congressional inquiry, specifically defined legislative investigation as a "limited" power, the limits being that the inquiry must be related to the powers expressly granted to Congress or "such auxiliary powers as are necessary and appropriate to make the express powers effective . . ." Because the powers of inquiry are limited, the Court went on, a witness before a congressional committee may "rightfully . . . refuse to answer where the bounds of the power are exceeded or the questions are not pertinent to the matter under inquiry."

The Watkins *Decision*

In the *Watkins* case a labor union official refused to answer questions put by the Un-American Activities Committee as to whether certain persons were members of the Communist Party. He agreed to testify concerning persons whom he believed to be active current communists, but refused to answer questions about former members who to his best knowledge had long since removed themselves from the movement. He contended that such questions were not authorized by law or relevant to the work of the committee; answers would accomplish no purpose except exposure of past activities. Two lower courts held Watkins guilty of contempt.

By a vote of 6 to 1 the Supreme Court reversed the conviction. The position taken by Chief Justice Warren in his opinion for the Court was subjected to much misrepresentation, partly, it must be admitted, because it was not so clear as it might have been. The basic proposition in the opinion was a reiteration of the well-established doctrine that the power of Congress to investigate, while broad, is not unlimited. What this means, Warren said, is that "there is no general authority to expose the private affairs of individuals without justification in terms of the functions of Congress." Moreover, no committee can act as a law-enforcement or trial agency. Under our system of separation of powers those are functions of the executive and judicial departments. The Chief Justice added at this point that "investigations conducted solely for the personal aggrandizement of the investigators or to 'punish' those investigated are indefensible." In short, "no inquiry is an end in itself; it must be related to and in furtherance of a legitimate task of Congress."

Having reasserted this general principle, the Chief Justice nevertheless found it unnecessary to examine the legitimacy of the Committee's purposes in questioning Watkins. While he had no doubt "that there is no congressional power to expose for the sake of exposure," Warren was understandably reluctant to get involved in ":esting the motives of committee members." Instead, Watkins was upheld on the more readily demonstrable proposition that the committee's investigatory authorization was unconstitutionally broad.

The Court ruled that in setting up committees or specifying their jurisdiction, the House or Senate must instruct the committee members "on what they are to do with the power delegated to them." The instructions to the committee must "spell out that group's jurisdiction and purpose with sufficient particularity" so that a witness and a reviewing court may have some basis for judging as to whether the questions asked are pertinent to the committee's legislative purpose. In addition to the pertinency test, such instructions are necessary if the House or Senate itself is to have any real responsibility for the committees which are purporting to act for the parent body.

In the *Watkins* case the Court held that the Un-American Activities Committee had failed this test. Its jurisdiction was stated by the House so broadly as to cover any subject it might conceivably wish to examine. Starting from an admittedly justifiable need by Congress to be informed of efforts to overthrow the government by force and violence so that adequate legislative safeguards could be erected, the committee had radiated outward "infinitely to any topic thought to be related in some way to armed insurrection."

There are many objections to running a committee in this freewheeling fashion, but the Supreme Court was particularly concerned in the *Watkins* case with the resulting threat to the First Amendment rights of witnesses. Chief Justice Warren wrote:

Clearly, an investigation is subject to the command that the Congress shall make no law abridging freedom of speech or press or assembly. . . . An investigation is part of lawmaking. . . . The

First Amendment may be invoked against infringement of the protected freedoms by law or by law-making.

How did such unrestrained inquiries as those of the Committee on Un-American Activities violate the First Amendment? Warren continued:

Abuses of the investigative process may imperceptibly lead to abridgement of protected freedoms. The mere summoning of a witness and compelling him to testify, against his will, about his beliefs, expressions or associations is a measure of governmental interference. And when those forced revelations concern matters that are unorthodox, unpopular, or even hateful to the general public, the reaction in the life of the witness may be disastrous.

A companion decision to *Watkins* was *Sweezy* v. *New Hampshire* (1957), in which the Court invalidated a state legislative inquiry by a 6 to 2 vote.[1] The New Hampshire legislature had constituted the attorney general of the state as a one-man legislative committee and directed him to determine whether there were in the state any "subversive persons" as defined in the state subversive activities law. Sweezy was twice subjected to sweeping inquiries into his activities and beliefs by the attorney general. Sweezy answered many questions, specifically denying that he had ever been a member of the Communist Party, but he refused to answer questions which he regarded as not pertinent to the subject under inquiry, as well as any questions about his opinions or beliefs.The contempt charge was based on his refusal to answer questions concerning his activities in the Progressive Party, which ran Henry Wallace for President in 1948, and the ideas he expressed in a guest lecture at the University of New Hampshire in 1954.

As in *Watkins*, the Chief Justice used some broad condemnatory language, but ultimately based his decision on the narrower ground of absence of legislative control over the use of the investigatory power. Justice Frankfurter, concurring, dealt with the more basic issue of the legislature's right to ask such questions, which he found unjustified in the circumstances of this proceeding.

As additional background for these two decisions, it should be

[1] The dissenters were Justices Burton and Clark.

recalled that the Court two years earlier had made a spirited defense of the right of a witness before a congressional committee to claim the Fifth Amendment. The cases were *Emspak* v. *United States* and *Quinn* v. *United States*, decided the same day in 1955. Both Quinn and Emspak had refused to answer questions before the Un-American Activities Committee, but their pleas under the Fifth Amendment had been "deliberately phrased in muffled terms." The government charged that they were trying to "obtain the benefit of the privilege without incurring the popular opprobrium which often attaches to its exercise." The Court majority, however, held that they had given adequate notice of their intention to invoke the privilege. Significantly, Chief Justice Warren said in the *Emspak* decision:

If it is true that in these times a stigma may somehow result from a witness' reliance on the Self-Incrimination Clause, a committee should be all the more ready to recognize a veiled claim of the privilege. Otherwise, the great right which the Clause was intended to secure might be effectively frustrated by private pressures.

The Court fully realized the risks it was running when it handed down decisions like these, and particularly the *Watkins* decision. In announcing its intention to protect the First Amendment rights of committee witnesses, the Chief Justice noted that the Court was assuming "an arduous and delicate task." It was also a task which brought the Court under violent criticism from Congress and many other influential sources of opinion throughout the country.

Congressional Reaction to Watkins

Congressional reaction to the *Watkins* decision was, first, the 1957 Jenner bill to withdraw from the appellate jurisdiction of the Supreme Court prosecutions for contempt of Congress. However, Senator Butler's 1958 amendments to the Jenner bill abandoned this tactic in favor of a considerably milder approach.[2] Butler explained his proposal to the Senate at length on August 20. Piercing through what he called the "sheer verbiage" of the *Watkins* opinion which "inundated . . . those who attempt to follow its logic," he concluded that the Court's finding was "that the scope of an investiga-

[2] S. 2646, 85th Cong., sec. 2.

tion had not been sufficiently defined to enable the witness to determine the pertinency of a question asked of him." The witness, according to the Court, "was entitled to know with certainty whether the question being asked him was pertinent, since in the criminal statute on contempt Congress had made pertinency a factor in the crime of contempt." [3]

This analysis of the opinion's reasoning seems substantially correct. The Court's decision proposed that the pertinency problem be solved by having Congress specify more clearly the limits of a committee's authority, and not make such vague and sweeping grants of jurisdiction as those which set the Un-American Activities Committee up in business. With a clearer authorization as the basis for a committee inquiry, then the witness and the reviewing court would be aided in determining the pertinency of specific questions. It should be noted that this is one area in which the Bar Association resolutions, reviewed in Chapter 2, accepted the Court's position and urged Congress to follow its advice. The A.B.A. resolution suggested that, to meet the problems created by the *Watkins* decision, "the quickest and best solution is for the House of Representatives to rewrite its resolution of authority to its Congressional Committee investigating internal security and Communist activities in terms so thoroughly, carefully and precisely worded as to leave no area for reasonable misunderstanding or evasion. . . ."

Senator Butler could not of course deal with the problems of a House committee. Rather, he sought to meet the *Watkins* problem by asserting legislative responsibility for decisions on pertinency. The issue of pertinency, he contended, could not be decided either by the witness or by a reviewing court. "Pertinency in the sense in which it is referred to here involves the legislative need for the information being sought, and this is a question to be determined by the legislative body, and not otherwise."

The Butler bill provided, first, that any question was to be deemed pertinent if its pertinency was not questioned by the witness. Second, if the point of pertinency was raised by the witness, the presiding officer of the committee would determine whether the question was

[3] *Congressional Record*, vol. 104, pp. 18658–9.

pertinent in the sense that there was a legislative need for the information sought to be elicited. This ruling would stand unless reversed on appeal from the ruling of the chair, and there could be a further consideration of the pertinency issue by the full House or Senate when either of these bodies was called upon to adopt a resolution initiating a criminal prosecution against the witness for contempt of Congress.

The purpose of the Butler plan was to give Congress the maximum amount of authority in decisions pertaining to the legitimate scope of its investigations. However, Butler denied that he was attempting to withdraw from the courts determination of the essential jurisdictional element in the crime of contempt of Congress. He emphasized that his proposal would leave with the courts the responsibility of determining whether the questions propounded by the committee were, in fact, within the jurisdiction of the committee.

The congressional committee would determine only the issue as to whether the question asked was pertinent to the issue under investigation. A witness could still protest that a committee was going outside its constitutional or delegated authority in investigating that issue, and could refuse to answer on that ground. It would then remain for the courts to decide whether the inquiry was within the scope of the committee's authority. Butler recognized that the responsibility for determining this question, which he called "jurisdictional pertinency," could not be withdrawn from the courts, for it was an essential element in the crime of contempt of Congress. He said specifically on this point:

I would not want to withdraw from the Court's consideration the issue of whether a question propounded by a Congressional committee was, in fact, within the jurisdiction of the committee. I do not want any committee of Congress to possess the power to summon persons, or to compel persons to submit documents and papers, or to answer questions, which that Committee, under its delegated authority, has no right to require. . . . I would deem such an attempt to be clearly unconstitutional.[4]

Senator Hennings summed up the objections to the Butler pro-

4 *Congressional Record*, vol. 104, p. 18658.

posal when he said that it would be "unwise if not unconstitutional" for Congress to make a final determination of *any* element going into the crime of contempt. "Congress has placed upon the Federal courts the duty of punishing for contempt of Congress. Pertinency of the question asked by a committee has been established by the Congress as an essential element of the crime. In my opinion, all elements of a crime should be decided judicially by the court and the jury." [5]

The Barenblatt *Decision*

The Butler bill did not pass in the 1958 session. Before similar legislation could get much attention during the 1959 session, the case for it was liquidated by the Court's retreat from the *Watkins* holding in *Barenblatt* v. *United States* (1959). The vote in *Barenblatt* was 5 to 4. The six-judge *Watkins* majority was reduced to a four-judge minority by the defection of Justices Harlan and Frankfurter. Joining them were Clark, who had been the sole dissenter in *Watkins*, Whittaker, who had not participated in *Watkins*, and Stewart, appointed after the *Watkins* decision.

Justice Harlan, who wrote the *Barenblatt* opinion, did not specifically overrule *Watkins*. In part he accomplished his result by distinguishing *Watkins* from *Barenblatt* on the difference in the facts of the two cases. What were the differences?

1. Watkins was a labor union official questioned on the subject of communism in labor, whereas Barenblatt was a college professor who was questioned in an inquiry into communism in education.

2. Watkins had testified to his own relationship with the Communist Party but had refused to answer questions about the past membership of other persons in the party, whereas the three counts on which the Supreme Court upheld Barenblatt's conviction were refusals to answer questions pertaining to his own present or past membership in the party.

3. In *Watkins* "the petitioner had made specific objection to the Subcommittee's questions on the ground of pertinency; the question under inquiry had not been disclosed in any illuminating manner;

[5] *Ibid.*, p. 18686.

48

and the questions asked the petitioner were not only amorphous on their face, but in some instances clearly foreign to the alleged subject matter of the investigation"; whereas Barenblatt "raised no objections on the ground of pertinency at the time any of the questions were put to him," and in any case pertinency was made to appear "with undisputable clarity."

There were also, of course, important similarities in the two cases, to which Harlan did not call attention. Barenblatt was before the same committee, which was operating under the same vague mandate and using the same tactics of exposure and publicity-seeking which the Court had castigated in *Watkins*.

Having established certain factual differences between the two cases, Harlan undertook as the second stage in his reasoning to minimize or render inapplicable the constitutional holding of *Watkins*. This was made somewhat more easy because, as already noted, the actual doctrine of the *Watkins* case was much more limited than Warren's bold language might have led one to think. Warren had apparently held the mandate of the committee to be unconstitutionally vague, so that it was impossible for a witness before the committee to determine whether questions asked were pertinent to the committee's legitimate legislative purpose. But according to Harlan's version, the Court had reversed Watkins' conviction "solely" on the ground that he had not been adequately apprised of the subject matter of the investigation, and the vagueness of the mandate was only one of the factors in this failure. If the committee adequately informed the witness in some other fashion of the purposes of its inquiry, then the vagueness of the mandate would not be a constitutional defect. Any other interpretation of *Watkins*, Harlan pointed out, would render the Un-American Activities Committee completely incapable of compelling testimony under any circumstance.

Certainly there were many who had interpreted the *Watkins* ruling to mean exactly that. The American Bar Association had apparently done so, for it had recommended that the House enact new legislation clearly specifying the committee's area of investigative interest. But the *Barenblatt* decision now released the House from any necessity of clarifying the jurisdiction of the committee. The rule under which the committee had been set up, Harlan said, "comes to us with a 'persuasive gloss of legislative history,' . . . which shows beyond doubt that in pursuance of its legislative concerns in the domain of 'national security' the House has clothed the Un-American Activities Committee with pervasive authority to investigate Communist activities in this country."

One may grant that Harlan was correct in holding that the House had by repeated actions indicated its support for the committee's wide-ranging investigations, yet still hold some doubt about his assumption that congressional or committee action can validate any vagueness of mandate. The Court in *Watkins* had condemned vagueness of mandate for two principal reasons. First, vagueness rendered it impossible for the parent body to exercise supervision over the committee. Harlan passed over this point in silence, presumably adopting for the *Barenblatt* majority the view that the degree of supervision Congress gives to its committees is its own business.

Second, vagueness of mandate makes it impossible for a witness, and later a reviewing court, to judge whether particular questions are pertinent to the legitimate concerns of the committee. Harlan did speak to this issue, and took care of it, as noted, by finding factual differences between Barenblatt's and Watkins' situations. As a reviewing judge he had no doubt that the committee's questions were pertinent to its announced subject of "Communist infiltration into the field of education."

Since the vagueness and pertinency issues, which had been determinative in *Watkins*, were thus disposed of, the Court proceeded to the ultimate question, which it had managed to talk about but not to reach in *Watkins* — namely, the applicability of the First Amendment. It had taken over twenty years since the Un-American Activities Committee first began to ask individuals about their connection with the Communist Party for the Court to come to grips with this problem. Now its answer was a strong affirmation of the superiority of congressional power over the protection of the First Amendment.

Congressional power to legislate in the field of communist activity, Harlan said, was undoubted. "In the last analysis this power rests

on the right of self-preservation, 'the ultimate value of any society.' "
Congress has proceeded on the assumption that the Communist
Party aims at overthrow of the government of the United States by
force and violence. The Court itself, Harlan went on, had in numerous decisions refused to consider the Communist Party "as an ordinary political party, and has upheld federal legislation aimed at the
Communist problem which in a different context would certainly
have raised constitutional issues of the gravest character." In balancing "the competing private and public interests at stake," the
public needs here were regarded by Harlan as real and urgent.

The fact that this particular inquiry impinged on the field of education did not condemn it, Harlan continued, and the *Sweezy* case
with its comments on the need for academic freedom was inapplicable. Sweezy was questioned about a lecture given at a university
and about his connection with the Progressive Party, which was on
the 1948 ballot in twenty-six states as a normal political party.
Barenblatt, identified by a previous committee witness as a one-time
member of the Communist Party, was questioned to throw light on
"the extent to which the Communist Party has succeeded in infiltrat-
ing into our universities, or elsewhere, persons and groups committed
to furthering the objectives of overthrow." Nor could the inquiry be
attacked as one aimed at "theoretical classroom discussion of communism." The difficult problem of determining when advocacy of
revolution may be constitutionally subjected to criminal prosecution, which Harlan himself had dealt with in the *Yates* case, was
irrelevant in a congressional investigation which of necessity "must
proceed step by step."

Finally, Harlan reached the "exposure" issue. One of Warren's
many dicta in *Watkins* was that "there is no congressional power to
expose for the sake of exposure," which he had promptly offset by
disclaiming any judicial intent to inquire into the "motives" of committee members. Consequently the way had been prepared for Harlan to say: "So long as Congress acts in pursuance of its constitutional power, the judiciary lacks authority to intervene on the basis
of the motives which spurred the exercise of that power." The Court
has of course occasionally questioned the motives of Congress. It

did so in a very explicit fashion in the famous *Child Labor Tax Case*.[6] But Justice Harlan chose as his peroration a quotation from a decision in which the Court denied its power to question motives, *McCray* v. *United States* (1904):

It is, of course, true that if there be no authority in the judiciary to restrain a lawful exercise of power by another department of the government, where a wrong motive or purpose has impelled to the exertion of the power, that abuses of a power conferred may be temporarily effectual. The remedy for this, however, lies, not in the abuse of the judicial authority of its functions, but in the people, upon whom, after all, under our institutions, reliance must be placed for the correction of abuses committed in the exercise of a lawful power.

Four members of the Court would not concede that "abuses" by legislative investigating committees touching the First Amendment rights of witnesses were beyond judicial authority to control. Justice Black wrote the principal dissent, in which Chief Justice Warren and Justice Douglas concurred, while Justice Brennan wrote a short dissent confined to the exposure issue.

Black had three main reasons for holding the committee action invalid. First, he stood on the *Watkins* holding about vagueness of the mandate, which Harlan had abandoned. Second, he declared that the committee action infringed the First Amendment. He attacked Harlan's "balancing" principle, saying that in effect it rewrote the First Amendment to read:

Congress shall pass no law abridging freedom of speech, press, assembly and petition, unless Congress and the Supreme Court reach the joint conclusion that on balance the interests of the Government in stifling these freedoms is greater than the interest of the people in having them exercised.

Even if balancing was a proper method of determining the meaning of the First Amendment, Black thought the majority had done it badly here. Harlan had balanced the right of the government to preserve itself against Barenblatt's right not to talk. What should have been thrown into the scale was the interest of society, of the people as a whole "in being able to join organizations, advocate

[6] *Bailey* v. *Drexel Furniture Co.* (1922).

52

causes and make political 'mistakes' without later being subjected to governmental penalties for having dared to think for themselves." On the other side of the scale, the congressional interest was vastly overstated as "self-preservation," with no mention that legislative power to make laws affecting speech and association is limited, and even less where education is concerned.

The majority opinion assumed, continued Black, that communists are not entitled to the protection of the First Amendment because "they do not constitute a political party but only a criminal gang." Such an assertion is in effect a declaration of outlawry of the party, whereas it has been the consistent policy of the Attorney General and the director of the FBI to advise against outlawing the party. If the Communist Party can be outlawed because some of its members are bad and some of its tenets are illegal, then "no group is safe." Black believed that the Communist Party could not be outlawed "as a group, without endangering the liberty of all of us."

Finally, Black contended that "the chief aim, purpose and practice" of the House committee was the illegal one of trying witnesses and punishing them "by humiliation and public shame." Black cited in proof of this intent the long history of committee practice, and concluded:

. . . the Court today fails to see what is here for all to see — that exposure and punishment is the aim of this Committee and the reason for its existence. To deny this aim is to ignore the Committee's own claims and the reports it has issued ever since it was established. I cannot believe that the nature of our judicial office requires us to be so blind, and must conclude that the Un-American Activities Committee's "identification" and "exposure" of Communists and suspected Communists, like the activities of the Committee in Kilbourn v. Thompson, amount to an encroachment on the judiciary which bodes ill for the liberties of the people of this land.

The Uphaus Decision

As the *Watkins* decision was distinguished almost to death by *Barenblatt*, so the *Sweezy* case received the same treatment in *Uphaus* v. *Wyman*. Here it was Justice Clark, by no means so skillful a practitioner as Harlan, who acted for the same five-judge majority.

Uphaus, a minister and a pacifist, was executive director of an organization called World Fellowship, Inc., which maintained a summer camp in New Hampshire. The attorney general of the state, acting as a one-man legislative investigating committee under the same statutory authorization to determine whether there were "subversive persons" in the state that was involved in the *Sweezy* case, demanded the names of all persons who had attended the camp over a two-year period. Uphaus refused to produce the guest list, and was convicted of civil contempt.

The Supreme Court's decision in the 1958 case of *National Association for the Advancement of Colored People* v. *Alabama* might have seemed to offer a certain parallel to the *Uphaus* problem. There the Court had unanimously denied the power of the state of Alabama to demand the production of its membership lists. The state alleged that the lists were necessary to permit determination whether the organization, chartered in New York, was unlawfully carrying on local activities within the state. But the Court concluded that compelled disclosure of affiliation with the group might well constitute a substantial restraint on freedom of association. Evidence indicated that in the past revelation of the identity of members had exposed them to economic reprisal, threat of physical coercion, and other manifestations of public hostility. Balancing these very probable consequences of disclosure against the need asserted by the state, the Court concluded that the state had failed to show any "substantiality of . . . interest" which would justify the limitation of constitutional freedom.

Clark distinguished *Uphaus* from the *NAACP* situation by finding a "substantiality" of interest in New Hampshire which had been lacking in Alabama. The legislature had commissioned the attorney general to determine the existence of "subversive persons" in the state. Evidence offered in court connected Uphaus with many "communist front" activities and indicated that at least nineteen speakers invited to talk at World Fellowship had either been members of the Communist Party or had connections with organizations on the United States Attorney General's list of subversive organizations. The state legislature had made a legislative finding that "subversive persons" posed a serious threat to the security of the state. Thus the investigation was undertaken to protect a basic governmental interest which outweighed rights in the "associational privacy" of a public camp furnishing board and lodging. The "exposure" to which persons who had been guests at the camp were subjected was simply "an inescapable incident of an investigation into the presence of subversive persons within a State."

Justice Brennan for the minority built a substantially tighter case for the exercise of judicial surveillance over legislative investigations than the Chief Justice had constructed in *Watkins* and *Sweezy*. He started with this basic proposition: either the courts have some responsibility for judging whether legislative investigations impinge on constitutionally protected rights, when such claims are raised by prosecutions for contempt of legislative committees, or they do not. The latter doctrine has never been accepted; as Brennan said, "this Court has rightly turned its back on the alternative of universal subordination of protected interests." Consequently, while the Court must be constantly aware of all the justifications for breadth of scope in legislative inquiries, it must also be conscious of "the inescapable judicial task in giving substantive content, legally enforced, to the Due Process Clause."

The majority opinion, Brennan contended, stated an entirely unacceptable standard for judicial judgment — whether "the investigation is rationally connected with a discernible legislative purpose." In contrast, he recalled the statement in *Watkins* "that the mere semblance of a legislative purpose would not justify an inquiry in the face of the Bill of Rights." He admitted that "preservation of the state's existence is undoubtedly a proper purpose for legislation," and for furthering by legislative investigation. "But, in descending from this peak of abstraction to the facts of this case, one must ask the question: What relation did this investigation of individual conduct have to legislative ends here?"

His analysis of the facts, in a search for a valid legislative end, disclosed "an investigation in which the processes of law-making and law-evaluating were submerged entirely in exposure of individual behavior — in adjudication, of a sort, however much disclaimed, through the exposure process." The emphasis of the report to the legislature prepared by the state attorney general was entirely on "individual guilt, individual near-guilt, and individual questionable behavior." The record showed that "the investigatory objective was the impermissible one of exposure for exposure's sake," which had been condemned in *Watkins*. While most legislative investigations unavoidably involve exposure of some sort, here "exposure was the very core, and deliberately and purposefully so, of the legislative investigation." This was, to quote *Kilbourn* v. *Thompson*, a classic example of "a fruitless investigation into the personal affairs of individuals."

The defense that the investigation must be presumed valid because "the precise shape of the legislative action" which might eventually be undertaken was necessarily unknown, seemed to Brennan to condemn itself. It amounted to the anomalous claim "that the vaguer the State's interest is, the more laxly will the Court view the matter and indulge a presumption of the existence of a valid subordinating state interest. In effect, a roving investigation and exposure of past associations and expressions in the political field is upheld because it might lead to some sort of legislation which might be sustained as constitutional, and the entire process is said to become the more defensible rather than the less because of the vagueness of the issues."

What Brennan asked was that the state make some "initial showing" that it would or could make some use of the kind of information it was demanding from Uphaus which would not invade his privacy and that of his guests as it related to freedom of speech and assembly. "If the principles this Court has announced, and to which the Court today makes some deference, are to have any meaning, it must be up to the State to make at least some plausible disclosure of its lawmaking interest so that the relevance of its inquiries to it may be tested." He concluded: "On any basis that has practical meaning, New Hampshire has not made such a showing here."

The *Barenblatt* and *Uphaus* decisions constituted notice to Congress and to the states that they need have no further concern about judicial limitations on investigatory powers. The brave words of

Watkins and *Sweezy* had been withdrawn. Where *Watkins* had said that "there is no congressional power to expose for the sake of exposure," *Uphaus* had rebutted, "exposure . . . is an inescapable incident of an investigation." Where *Watkins* had said, "We cannot simply assume . . . that every congressional investigation is justified by a public need that overbalances any private rights affected," *Uphaus* asserted there was no judicial alternative but acquiescence in the "legislative determination that [subversive] persons, statutorily defined with a view toward the Communist Party, posed a serious threat to the security of the State." Where in *Watkins* and *Sweezy* the Court had shown some willingness to look at the actual conduct of the investigators and to draw some obvious conclusions as to the nature of their interests, in *Barenblatt* and *Uphaus* the Court was that "blind" Court, against which Chief Justice Taft admonished in a famous passage, that does not see what "all others can see and understand."

The major objection to the *Barenblatt* decision, however, is not so much its liquidation or limitation of *Watkins*, for in perspective it is clear that *Watkins* was not much of a decision. While talking a lot about fundamental problems of congressional investigatory power, the Court finally settled on the comparatively minor problem of pertinency as the issue on which to decide the *Watkins* case. As the pertinency rule was applied in *Barenblatt*, the relevance of legislative questions to legislative purposes will be very easy to demonstrate. Only in cases where the interrogators are singularly stupid, as in fact they were in the Virginia inquiry invalidated by the Court in *Scull* v. *Virginia* (1959), will the pertinency rule be any protection to committee witnesses.

The real tragedy of *Barenblatt* is that the Court again fumbled an opportunity to develop a theory of judicial control which in practice would take account of the need to safeguard both legislative rights to decide what information is needed and private rights against coercion and humiliation. The Court saw only two alternatives. One was to assert judicial veto power over the substance of legislative inquiries and the motives of the inquirers, which it rejected with good cause. The other was to express a mild judicial interest in procedural

57

problems such as pertinency. The Court accepted this latter approach, but it is far from meeting the real problem.

The Court has never considered a third possibility, recently suggested by Harry Kalven and Alexander Meiklejohn.[7] Briefly, their proposal is that a distinction be made between the power of Congress to investigate in aid of legislation and the power of Congress to compel testimony for this purpose. The Court, along with almost everyone else, has assumed that the two powers must be coextensive, because Congress must be able to force relevant information from hostile and reluctant witnesses. Kalven and Meiklejohn suggest that in fact the power to compel testimony should be far narrower than the power to investigate, on the theory that information forced from witnesses is inevitably factual detail about individual conduct or actions which cannot possibly be of much real use to Congress in developing general legislative policies. As Kalven says, it is surely absurd to assume that the best route to legislative insight into the problem of dealing with internal subversion "is to inventory the Communists in the United States one at a time," as several committees have been doing at great cost to individual privacy.

Any judicial effort to announce and to work out the application of a rule for narrowing legislative power to compel testimony would admittedly be a task of major proportions, but some creative judicial statesmanship is called for to rescue the Court from its present stalemate on the congressional investigation issue. In *Watkins* the Court marched up the hill, and in *Barenblatt* it marched back down. Judicial prestige is not promoted by such a performance.

[7] Harry Kalven, Jr., "Mr. Alexander Meiklejohn and the Barenblatt Opinion," and Alexander Meiklejohn, "The Barenblatt Opinion," 27 *University of Chicago Law Review* 315–340 (1960).

5

ЛЛЛЛЛЛЛЛЛЛЛЛЛЛЛЛЛЛЛЛЛ

THE SMITH ACT
ISSUE

THE Smith Act, adopted in 1940, makes it unlawful knowingly to advocate or teach the overthrow of any government in the United States by force or violence, to print or distribute written matter so advocating, or to organize or knowingly to become a member of any group which so advocates. These are the provisions of section 2. Section 3 goes on to make conspiracy to accomplish any of these ends also punishable.

In *Dennis* v. *United States* (1951), a prosecution under section 3, the Supreme Court construed the Smith Act for the first time, under a limited grant of certiorari which permitted the Court to consider only the issue of constitutionality. The Court held the act to be constitutional, and affirmed the convictions of eleven leaders of the American Communist Party. This success led the government to bring many additional prosecutions against communists under section 3 of the act, in which it was almost uniformly successful.

The Supreme Court refused for several years to grant certiorari to review any of these convictions. When it finally agreed to take the case of *Yates* v. *United States* in 1955, involving the conviction of fourteen communists in California, it granted certiorari without this time imposing any limitation on its review. When the Court decided the case in 1957, it did not question the constitutionality of the Smith Act as established by the *Dennis* ruling, but it did look at issues of statutory interpretation, procedure, and evidence which led it to reverse the convictions of five defendants and to grant new trials to the other nine. The Department of Justice subsequently abandoned prosecutions under section 3 of the act for the apparent reason that it could not meet the standards of proof required by the *Yates* decision.

Interpretation of "Organize"

One of the principal grounds on which the Court relied in deciding the *Yates* case was an issue of statutory interpretation, which concerned the meaning of the term "organize" in the statute. The Smith Act provides criminal punishment for anyone who "organizes or helps to organize any society, group, or assembly of persons who teach, advocate, or encourage the overthrow or destruction" of government in the United States by force or violence. The defendants, who were charged under the Smith Act with organizing the Communist Party of the United States, contended that "organize" must be interpreted to mean "establish" or "bring into existence," and that in this sense the Communist Party had been organized by 1945 at the latest. The chronology was that the American Communist Party had been originally founded in 1919. In 1941 the party had been liquidated and replaced by the so-called Communist Political Association, this change purporting to establish the surrender of the political goals of the group. In 1945, however, the Communist Party was re-established on the earlier model.

The reason why the meaning of "organize" and the date of "organization" of the party were important was because of the operation of the three-year statute of limitations on criminal prosecutions. If the party had been "organized" in 1945, then the indictment in the *Yates* case, returned in 1951, was barred by the statute of limitations. To avoid such a holding, the government argued that "organize" should be given a broader meaning. Organizing, it was contended, is a continuing process that does not end until the entity is dissolved. New cells or units are continually being "organized," and "organizers" are constantly active in securing new members.

In deciding against the government's contention Justice Harlan, writing for the majority, relied on one of the Court's earliest rules of statutory interpretation, the principle that penal laws are to be construed strictly. This rule, as Chief Justice Marshall had said in an early case, "is founded on the tenderness of the law for the rights of individuals; and on the plain principle that the power of punishment is vested in the legislative, not in the judicial department. It is the legislature, not the Court, which is to define a crime, and ordain its punishment."[1] Thus the narrow interpretation of "organize" — subsequently attacked in Congress and elsewhere as judicial legislation — was actually grounded, according to Harlan, in a desire to do as little judicial legislating as possible.

The arguments for a broader interpretation of "organize," as urged by the government, would have required the Court to rely on some of the familiar devices for reading meaning into statutory language. "Congressional intent" was appealed to in attacking the Court's interpretation. It was argued that Congress, adopting the Smith Act in 1940, would not have been intending to use "organize" in such a way as to make it inapplicable to the Communist Party, which had been founded in 1919. It was only the fact that the party was dissolved after 1940 and then "organized" anew in 1945 which gave this provision of the Smith Act, under Harlan's interpretation, any effectiveness at all against the Communist Party, and then only for a three-year period expiring in 1948. Congress, it was argued, would never have intended to frustrate in this way a statute which was aimed primarily at the Communist Party.

Justice Harlan, in rebuttal, answered that the Court could not presume the Smith Act was written only with the Communist Party in mind. The act covered also anarchists and syndicalists, and "was aimed equally at all groups falling within its scope." There were other provisions of the act, he pointed out, which were applicable to organizations already existing in 1940, such as the Communist Party, particularly the "advocating and teaching" language. Thus no gap in the act's coverage resulted from interpreting the "organization" provision to apply only to new organizations.

Dictionary definitions would support either of the two meanings

[1] *United States* v. *Wiltberger* (1820).

61

which were urged. And so the Court felt obliged to eschew any extrinsic aids to statutory construction, and to fall back on the familiar rule of strict construction of criminal statutes. In so doing, Justice Harlan concluded, the Court was reading the statute "according to the natural and obvious import of the language, without resorting to subtle and forced construction for the purpose of either limiting or extending its operation." [2]

Justices Burton and Clark disagreed with the Court on the meaning of "organize," Clark noting: "This construction frustrates the purpose of the Congress for the Act was passed in 1940 primarily to curb the growing strength and activity of the Party." Clark's position in essence was that the intent of Congress was to legislate against the Communist Party, and consequently that the interpretation of the legislation most unfavorable to the party should be accepted as the meaning of the language.

Efforts were immediately undertaken in Congress to amend the Smith Act in order to reverse the Court's interpretation and establish as congressional intent the broader definition of "organize." Among other efforts, this result was sought by section 4 of the Jenner-Butler bill which Congress considered during the 1958 session. Senator Butler said in arguing for this provision:

If we let the Smith Act stand on the books as it is today with the interpretation and application which the Supreme Court has given it in the Yates-Schneiderman decision, we shall be making it clear that we do not want the act to apply to the current activities of the Communist conspiracy in this country.[3]

After failure in the 85th Congress, a renewed effort was made in the 86th Congress to write an expanded definition of "organize" into the Smith Act, and the House without objection passed such a measure on March 2, 1959.[4] This was the language of the amendment:

As used in this section the term "organize," with respect to any society, group, or assembly of persons, includes the recruiting of new members, the forming of new units, and the regrouping or expansion

---

[2] Quoted from the opinion in *United States* v. *Temple* (1882).
[3] *Congressional Record*, vol. 104, p. 18662.
[4] H. R. 2369, 86th Cong.; *Congressional Record*, vol. 105, p. 3157.

of existing clubs, classes, and other units of such society, group, or assembly of persons.

However, the Senate took no action on the proposal.[5]

Advocacy and Unlawful Action

The other principal ground on which the *Yates* decision was based involves some constitutional analysis, which cannot be understood without knowing what the Court had done six years earlier when it decided *Dennis* v. *United States*. In the *Dennis* case upholding the constitutionality of the Smith Act, there were two respects in which the handling of the issues was inadequate. First, the Court in granting certiorari limited its review to questions of constitutionality of the statute, "inherently or as construed and applied in the instant case." Consequently the Court did not consider any of the questions about the nature or sufficiency of evidence presented to justify the findings of guilt under the statute or the trial judge's conclusions as to the extent of the danger posed by the Communist Party.

Second, in its dealing with the basic constitutional issue, the Court's opinion, written by Chief Justice Vinson, was less clear than it might have been. The indictment under the Smith Act charged the eleven communists with knowingly conspiring to organize a group to teach and advocate the overthrow and destruction of the government of the United States by force and violence. No overt revolutionary acts other than teaching and advocating were alleged. The major constitutional issue before the Court was how to reconcile with the free speech guarantee of the Constitution, convictions which treated speaking and teaching as criminal offenses.

Vinson's opinion partially solved the problem by dealing with speech as "advocacy" of unlawful action, but even so it was necessary to establish some relation between the advocacy and the possibility of action's occurring as a result of the advocacy. The classic method for establishing this relationship had been the "clear and present danger" test developed by Justices Holmes and Brandeis.

[5] The Dodd-Keating bill, S. 2652, reported out by the Senate Judiciary Committee during the 1960 session, contained a similar provision, but the bill was not called up for debate.

63

Stated summarily, the clear and present danger test would require a court to invalidate statutes punishing advocacy of overthrow of the government as enforced against allegedly subversive activities, unless the likelihood of success for the subversive activity was immediate and pressing.

Vinson in the *Dennis* decision abandoned this test in favor of a formula used by Judge Learned Hand in the court of appeals when it reviewed the *Dennis* convictions: "Whether the gravity of the 'evil,' discounted by its improbability, justifies such invasion of free speech as is necessary to avoid the danger." Using this test, Vinson rejected the contention "that success or probability of success is the criterion." Thus the opinion made it easier to treat advocacy as a crime. What was not sufficiently clear, however, was that the Court was placing this view of the dangers of advocacy within the context of possibilities of action presented by the circumstances and in the organizational setting of this case.

It was these two weaknesses of the *Dennis* ruling which caused the trouble in *Yates* v. *United States*. Justice Harlan's opinion for the Court, apart from the problem of statutory construction which has already been discussed, turned on two constitutional issues. The first grew out of the failure of the *Yates* trial judge in his instructions to the jury to distinguish adequately between "advocacy of abstract doctrine and advocacy directed at promoting unlawful action." The judge had apparently been misled by the looseness of some of Vinson's language into thinking that punishment of the advocacy of abstract doctrine was permissible under the First Amendment. His holding was that "mere doctrinal justification of forcible overthrow, if engaged in with the intent to accomplish overthrow, is punishable *per se* under the Smith Act." That sort of advocacy, replied Harlan, "even though uttered with the hope that it may ultimately lead to violent revolution, is too remote from concrete action to be regarded as the kind of indoctrination preparatory to action which was condemned in *Dennis*."

Harlan endeavored to restate the *Dennis* doctrine in a way that would make clear that Vinson was talking about "advocacy . . .

aimed at building up a seditious group and maintaining it in readiness for action at a propitious time." Harlan continued:

The essence of the *Dennis* holding was that indoctrination of a group in preparation for future violent action, as well as exhortation to immediate action, by advocacy found to be directed to "action for the accomplishment" of forcible overthrow, to violence "as a rule or principle of action," and employing "language of incitement" . . . is not constitutionally protected when the group is of sufficient size and cohesiveness, is sufficiently oriented towards action, and other circumstances are such as reasonably to justify apprehension that action will occur.

Because the trial judge had not understood this point and had failed to instruct the jury on the need to distinguish between advocacy of abstract doctrine and advocacy directed at promoting unlawful action, he had furnished the jury with "wholly inadequate guidance" on the central point in the case, requiring reversal of the convictions.

Justice Harlan's second problem was with the evidence on which the convictions had been secured. In pursuance of the holding just noted, the Court examined the evidence presented by the government to see whether it proved the charge of advocacy aimed at unlawful action. Evidence of advocacy was valueless if its effect was only to prove advocacy of the abstract doctrine of forcible overthrow. There had to be evidence of "Party advocacy or teaching in the sense of a call to forcible action at some future time."

In such evidence the Court found the record "strikingly deficient." The government's theory was that the Marxist-Leninist texts which it offered in evidence demonstrated the conspiratorial character of the Communist Party, and that conspiracy on the part of the defendants was proved by then connecting them with the party. This was easy, because they were all admittedly active in the party. But Harlan insisted that the party's advocacy of forcible action had to be shown by acts, not texts.

At best this voluminous record shows but a half dozen or so scattered incidents which, even under the loosest standards, could be deemed to show such advocacy. Most of these were not connected with any of the petitioners, or occurred many years before the period

65

covered by the indictment. We are unable to regard this sporadic showing as sufficient to justify viewing the Communist Party as the nexus between these petitioners and the conspiracy charged.

What the Court was saying was that evidence of activity in the Communist Party would not meet the requirements in this case. Some of the party's activities might be wholly lawful. The defendants could be convicted only on the basis of their individual acts other than their mere relations with the party. On this basis five of the defendants were completely cleared. There was no evidence in the record to connect them with the conspiracy charged except that they had long been members and officers of the Communist Party of California.

As for the other nine defendants, the Court was not prepared to go so far. There was evidence involving them — party classes, an "underground apparatus," board meetings held in a devious and conspiratorial manner — which might meet the Court's tests. "We are not prepared to say, at this stage of the case, that it would be impossible for a jury, resolving all conflicts in favor of the Government and giving the evidence . . . its utmost sweep, to find that advocacy of action was also engaged in when the group involved was thought particularly trustworthy, dedicated, and suited for violent tasks." The Court was here leaning over backward to find some shred of basis for giving weight to the government's case.

The End of Section 3 Prosecutions

The *Yates* decision was bitterly criticized because it kept a number of admitted communists from going to jail under the Smith Act. But it did not declare the Smith Act unconstitutional. In fact, Harlan clearly pointed out to the government what it must do if it wanted to send communists to jail under the act — namely, present in court some evidence of their conspiratorial activities other than reading books or making speeches. The Court recognized, as anyone who knows the history of sedition legislation in the United States must know, that the Smith Act challenges the First Amendment by making teaching and advocacy a crime. The government was happy to use the Smith Act against communists, instead of some of the other security

66

legislation on the books, because it is easy to prove that communists have made communist speeches and read communist books.

The Court went as far as it constitutionally could when in the *Dennis* case it conceded that speech can be punished, in spite of the First Amendment, when it is intimately connected with the possibility of action threatening the security of the nation. But because the First Amendment is involved, the Court could not abdicate its responsibility to judge whether there had been proof by judicial standards that the speech which was the basis of the offense had taken place in a framework of possible action, which alone could justify punishment for using the freedom guaranteed by the First Amendment. This is what the Court held that the government had failed to do in the *Yates* case.

The *Yates* decision brought to an apparent end an era of Smith Act prosecutions, in which verdicts of guilty had been almost automatically secured against any communist the government chose to bring into court. The decision served notice on the government that it could no longer convict communists by reading communist literature to juries. There had to be some evidence connecting the defendants to conspiratorial action. After a period of consideration, the Department of Justice dropped its case against the nine *Yates* defendants who had been granted new trials by the Supreme Court, as well as all other section 3 prosecutions. Presumably the Department concluded that the exposure of its operatives which would be involved by presenting them as witnesses in court was not worth the results achieved in jailing communists.

The Department of Justice, moreover, had had some painful experiences with paid anti-communist witnesses in its previous prosecutions. In *Communist Party* v. *Subversive Activities Control Board* (1956) the Supreme Court reversed a finding by the Board that the Communist Party was a "Communist-action organization" because of perjury by three of the government's paid ex-communist witnesses. Similarly in *Mesarosh* v. *United States* (1956) the Court ordered a new trial for three persons convicted in Pennsylvania of violating the Smith Act, because of the government's own subsequent doubts about the credibility of one of its witnesses.

67

The Status of Section 2

The only Smith Act problems remaining on the Court's agenda by 1960 were two cases testing section 2, the so-called membership section of the act, which makes criminal mere membership in a group advocating the overthrow of the government by force and violence. That the Court was having difficulty in resolving the constitutional questions raised by these cases was apparent from the almost unprecedented manner of their treatment.

Certiorari was granted in the first of these prosecutions against Junius Scales in March, 1956. The case was argued in October of that year, held under advisement to the end of the term in 1957, and then put over to the next term for reargument. At that time it was remanded to the trial court on motion of the Solicitor General, because of the possible impact of the *Jencks* decision. On retrial, Scales was again convicted, and certiorari was granted in December, 1958. The case was argued, but in June, 1959, it was reset for the next term. In October, 1959, the Court granted certiorari in a second case raising the same issue, *Noto* v. *United States*, and both cases were put over to February, 1960, for argument. On February 5 the Court, over the bitter dissent of Justice Clark, reset the two cases for argument on October 10, 1960, so that a third case, involving the registration of the Communist Party under the Internal Security Act, could be heard at the same time. Justice Clark pointed out that this meant the *Scales* case would have been on the docket for five terms and have received three arguments, and added: "I have found no appellate case in the history of the Court that has been carried on the active docket so many consecutive Terms or argued so often."

The Bar Association Proposal

It should be noted that the American Bar Association in its resolutions of February, 1959, urged Congress to reverse the constitutional position taken by the Court in the *Yates* case. The Bar Association proposed the following course of action:

Amend the Smith Act to make it a crime intentionally to advocate the violent overthrow of the Government of the United States or to teach the necessity, desirability, or duty of seeking to bring about such overthrow; in order that (1) this nation might take protective steps to prevent acts which, if not prevented, could result in bloodshed and treachery; and (2) this nation need not be forced to delay the invoking of the judicial process until such time as the resulting damage has already been wrought.

The two purposes which the Bar Association intended to achieve by this amendment are of course purposes which will be generally supported. But it does not follow that such an amendment was required to achieve them, or that the Supreme Court's rulings did in fact stand in the way of effective preventive measures against communist subversion. The resolution was particularly misleading in claiming that the *Yates* decision required delay in invoking the judicial process "until such time as the resulting damage has already been wrought."

The *Dennis* decision specifically spoke to this point. Chief Justice Vinson held there that the clear and present danger test "cannot mean that before the Government may act, it must wait until the *putsch* is about to be executed, the plans have been laid and the signal is awaited." The *Yates* decision did not weaken this position. Harlan's opinion permits the government to bring communists into court under the Smith Act before their actions have resulted in "damage" or "bloodshed." It imposes only two obligations on prosecutors of communists. First, the trial judge must charge the jury in the same language that Judge Medina used in the *Dennis* trial, or he must in other language make the same distinction that Judge Medina made between advocacy of abstract doctrine and advocacy directed at promoting unlawful action. Second, the prosecution must present proof linking the individuals on trial personally with party advocacy or teaching in the sense of a call to forcible action at some future time.

The Bar Association was apparently unwilling to accept these two limitations on the process of convicting communists. It proposed by legislation to make it unnecessary to show any connection between advocacy and unlawful action. The purpose of the language they proposed was to make certain kinds of speech a crime, regardless of their relationship to any possible action. It is highly regrettable that

69

persons presuming to speak for the organized American bar should have proposed legislation so patently contrary to American traditions of free speech and to the plain language of the Constitution. What does the First Amendment say? "Congress shall make no law . . . abridging the freedom of speech."

In 1798 Congress passed a sedition law, comparable in spirit to the measure the Bar Association proposed. It never was tested by the Supreme Court before it expired in 1801, but Jefferson said it was unconstitutional, and its infamous reputation in American history is well established. Subsequent sedition legislation — the Espionage Act of 1917, the Sedition Act of 1918, the Smith Act of 1940 — has been upheld by the Supreme Court, but always the justification for permitting speech to be punished has been its relation to unlawful action.

This was the whole purpose of the "clear and present danger" test. Justice Holmes was prepared to admit that the First Amendment did not prevent the community from protecting itself against danger resulting from speech. The Court, he said, must recognize that "When a nation is at war many things that might be said in time of peace are such a hindrance to its effort that their utterance will not be endured so long as men fight and that no Court could regard them as protected by any constitutional right." But he did not conclude that *any* legislative proscription of speech alleged to be dangerous was thereby constitutional. The speech had to meet the clear and present danger test before it could be constitutionally punished.

"The question," he said in *Schenck* v. *United States* (1919), "in every case is whether the words used are used in such circumstances and are of such a nature as to create a clear and present danger that they will bring about the substantive evils that Congress has a right to prevent. It is a question of proximity and degree." All subsequent Supreme Court discussion has proceeded on these same general assumptions. Even Vinson in the *Dennis* case, though he was willing to accept more remote standards of proximity and degree, was still relying upon the relationship to eventual action to hold the Smith Act constitutional.

In asserting the power of Congress to punish speech as a crime, without regard to the circumstances or to the organizational setting of the speech, the American Bar Association was proposing that Congress pass a clearly unconstitutional statute. It is a tribute to the common sense and the constitutional understanding of Congress that none of the numerous bills introduced to achieve the same purpose as that of the Bar Association proposal ever came close to adoption in either House.

6

⌐⌐⌐⌐⌐⌐⌐⌐⌐⌐⌐⌐⌐⌐⌐⌐⌐⌐⌐⌐⌐⌐⌐

THE PREEMPTION
ISSUE

In *Pennsylvania* v. *Nelson* (1956) the Supreme Court majority held that federal legislation, particularly the Smith Act, had "preempted" the field of protecting the United States against sedition, and had left the states with no power in this area. The *Nelson* case thus took its place in a long line of preemption decisions stretching back almost to the beginning of the nation. With two levels of government sharing many of the common public concerns over the same area, it often happens that both Congress and the state legislatures legislate on the same subject. It then becomes a responsibility for the courts, as these laws are brought into operation, to deal with any conflicts between them.

The state statutes must of course pass the test of constitutionality, just as the federal statutes must. But even if there is a valid constitutional basis for a state law, it may still be refused enforcement by the courts on the ground that it is in direct and necessary conflict with a valid federal law, or that Congress had by legislation in the same general area manifested an intention to occupy this field to the exclusion of any state legislation. It was this kind of a finding which the Supreme Court made in the *Nelson* case.

The Policy Issue in the Nelson Case

The great bulk of the Court's preemption holdings prior to *Nelson* had concerned state economic regulatory schemes which had been

72

invalidated because of conflict with federal legislation enacted under the commerce clause. In fact, the preemption doctrine had been largely developed in such cases. There had been exceptions, however. One of these, which provided the Court's principal reliance in the *Nelson* case, was *Hines* v. *Davidowitz* (1941), in which the federal Alien Registration Act of 1940 was held to supersede a Pennsylvania alien registration statute. However, in the *Hines* case the two statutes had certain conflicting provisions which made it relatively easy to find the state statute contrary to the congressional purpose. For example, the state law required aliens to carry identification cards at all times, an annoying obligation which Congress had considered and rejected in passing the federal law. In the *Nelson* case there was no substantial conflict between the federal and state laws. Rather, the Court rested its conclusion on the ground that Congress had so clearly manifested its intent to assume the responsibility of protecting the United States against subversion that state efforts toward the same end would have to be declared invalid.

Chief Justice Warren, writing the *Nelson* opinion, drew from the Court's previous decisions three tests of supercession — the "pervasiveness" of the federal scheme of regulation, the "dominance" of the federal interest, and the seriousness of the danger of conflict between federal and state schemes — and found each test was met in the current situation. Certainly the Smith Act, the Internal Security Act of 1950, and the Communist Control Act of 1954, added to numerous earlier federal statutes, did seem to meet the pervasive test. And it would be hard to deny that the national government has a dominant interest in protecting itself and the states from subversive overthrow. The seriousness of possible conflicts in concurrent enforcement of these statutes was rather less conclusively demonstrated. Hypothetical contingencies were mentioned, but no actual conflicts had occurred, and the Department of Justice specifically stated that the state legislation had not impeded federal enforcement.

Perhaps the most vulnerable part of the Court's argument on intent, however, was its treatment of the so-called saving clause in Section 3231 of the Criminal Code. This section provides:

The district courts of the United States shall have original juris-

73

diction, exclusive of the courts of the States, of all offenses against the laws of the United States.

Nothing in this title shall be held to take away or impair the jurisdiction of the courts of the several States under the laws thereof.

The Smith Act is included in the Criminal Code and is subject to this section, whatever it means. The Court, in a footnote to its opinion, held that the second sentence in Section 3231 was intended only to limit the jurisdictional grant made by the first sentence, and was not intended "to resolve particular supercession questions." This interpretation, however, does seem contrary to the plain language of the saving clause, and also contrary to a previous Supreme Court interpretation of its effect.[1] The *Nelson* minority considered that the effect of the language was to preserve the power of the states, even after the Smith Act, to adopt and enforce sedition acts, and thought that this point was sufficient in itself to decide the case.

By giving only a limited meaning to the saving clause, it will be noted, the Court preserved for itself the maximum opportunity for flexibility and adjustment in the rendering of judicial judgments on supercession problems. "Legislative intent" was assumed to vary in different situations, with the Court retaining responsibility for determining legislative intent as each statutory conflict came along. Now the plain fact is that in all the hard cases, which are the kind that get to the Supreme Court, the legislative intent cannot be determined with any degree of certainty, usually because Congress never thought about the conflict or expressed a conclusion about it in any coherent or authoritative fashion. Under these circumstances the Court may tend to find that the legislature did intend what it thinks the legislature should have intended.

By disposing of a controversy on the ground of legislative intent, moreover, the Supreme Court may be able to avoid or at least postpone taking a position on constitutional issues. This is what happened in the *Nelson* case. The Court made the case turn on the question whether Congress meant for the states to retain the power of punishing sedition against the United States. This holding made it unnecessary for the Court to consider, as it might have done, a ruling

[1] *Sexton v. California* (1903).

that the states have no constitutional power to punish sedition against the United States because this matter is of such vital and overwhelming concern to the nation that it must be exclusively handled by the nation. It has been argued with some authority that the states cannot punish treason against the United States.[2] Could it not well be contended that sedition against the United States is a comparable problem?

Consider the relevance of *Hines* v. *Davidowitz* on this point. The Court noted there, as a secondary consideration, that for the states to assume responsibilities for the control of aliens might cause the national government embarrassment in relations with foreign powers, a matter which is exclusively a national concern. If the state law in the *Hines* case had not been condemned by its conflict with the federal alien registration statute, the Court could have struck it down simply as a state intervention in an exclusively federal function. But legislative intention supplied a non-constitutional route to the same result, and the Court used the same route in *Nelson*.

The *Nelson* ruling was concerned only with state prosecutions which charged sedition against the United States. The Court left the states free to prosecute for sedition involving their own safety and for local breaches of the peace in connection with any sedition efforts. There was some uncertainty on this point, but it was made clear by an incidental statement of Justice Clark's in the 1959 *Uphaus* decision. The *Nelson* opinion, he affirmed, only prohibited the states from punishing "the same conduct" that was proscribed by the Smith Act. It did not strip the states "of the right to protect themselves" or to prosecute "for sedition against the state itself." It only forbade "a race between Federal and state prosecutors to the courthouse door."

As thus authoritatively interpreted, the *Nelson* decision constitutes a rational division of the responsibility for protection against subversion, a division justified by the most cogent reasons of public policy. It would be naive not to think that such policy considerations

[2] See Roger C. Cramton, "Supercession and Subversion: Limitations on State Power to Deal with Issues of Subversion and Loyalty," 8 *University of Chicago Law School Record* 33 (1958), and cases there cited.

had an influence on the Court. In fact, the Warren opinion plainly stated several grounds for judicial unhappiness with state sedition laws in general and the Pennsylvania statute in particular.

Many of the state laws, the Court said, were "vague and almost wholly without . . . safeguards." One of the provisions of the Pennsylvania act was "strangely reminiscent of the Sedition Act of 1798." The fact that a prosecution could be initiated under the act by a private individual, the Chief Justice noted, "presents a peculiar danger of interference with the federal program" and provided an opportunity "for the indulgence of personal spite and hatred or for furthering some selfish advantage or ambition." The Court also laid great stress on the possibility of double punishment by reason of parallel federal and state laws.

Each of these points, which were merely mentioned in the Court's opinion, could have been developed more fully. The reference to the infamous Sedition Act of 1798, for example, serves as a reminder of the general suspicion and distaste which the United States has traditionally had for such sedition acts, which deal in the dangerous business of levying punishment on speech and beliefs. Unless these statutes are narrowly drawn and unless their enforcement proceeds with due recognition of the various problems of freedom of speech inevitably involved in every prosecution, infringement of the First Amendment is very likely. If the states are to engage in the business of prosecuting for alleged seditious activities against the United States, the burden will be imposed on the Supreme Court of examining every such statute for constitutional conformity, with the same degree of care employed for the federal Smith Act in the *Dennis* case.

Assuming the state statutes pass the test of constitutionality, the task would remain of examining each conviction thereunder with the same care as in the *Yates* case to determine whether there had been due conformity to the requirements of evidence and proof. Because these sedition prosecutions involve bitterly disliked political minorities and dissenters, the trials are usually surrounded by conditions of passion and hysteria, and juries are almost certain to convict on any kind of evidence. Consequently the problem of an appellate court which endeavors to guarantee full constitutional rights even to communists will be particularly difficult in reviewing sedition convictions.

There is another policy reason against state sedition laws, and that is the complete failure to demonstrate that they are needed or that attempts to enforce them would serve any useful purpose. The program of communist subversion within the United States, while its effectiveness is often much exaggerated, nevertheless deserves to be met at the highest level and by use of the nation's best resources. Basic strategy decisions must be made, on such matters as whether it is preferable, at a given time, to have American communist leaders at large or in jail; whether it is preferable to allow the Communist Party (well infiltrated by government agents) to operate with a certain degree of freedom, or to undertake a vigorous policy of suppression which will inevitably drive the party workers underground.

These decisions must be made by the Department of Justice and the FBI. It is true that the Department of Justice took the position in a brief submitted as a friend of the Court in the *Nelson* case that state sedition legislation had not impeded federal enforcement of the Smith Act. But perhaps the reason for this is the fact that there had been almost no prosecutions under state laws. It is inconceivable that state action could ever be a major reliance against subversive movements of national importance. The state's role is almost certain to be that of supplying handy weapons for ambitious local politicians and for undertaking reprisals against unpopular groups or persons.

The Supreme Court, however, was careful to avoid resting its *Nelson* decision on such controversial policy considerations. Instead, it followed the long-standing judicial practice of deciding a case on statutory rather than constitutional grounds wherever possible. In determining that Congress had intended to occupy the field of punishing sedition against the federal government, the Court may conceivably have misinterpreted such congressional intent as had been expressed on the subject. It is significant, however, that congressional efforts to reverse the Court's "misinterpretation" failed in both the 1958 and 1959 sessions of Congress. Should Congress subsequently restore the state sedition statutes to effectiveness by appropriate legislation, then the first state prosecution for sedition against the United States which reaches the Supreme Court will force consideration of the constitutional issues which the Court avoided in the *Nelson* case.

The Effort to Adopt H. R. 3

The *Nelson* decision aroused some members of Congress to attempt not only to reverse the specific *Nelson* holding on state sedition laws, but also to adopt new legislation laying down broad principles binding on the Court in its adjudication of all federal-state conflicts. The principal effort of this sort was that embodied in the measure drafted by Representative Smith of Virginia, which had the number of H. R. 3 in both the 85th and 86th Congresses. As already noted, H. R. 3 easily passed the House in 1958, but in the Senate was defeated by a motion to recommit, adopted by a vote of 41 to 40. In the 1959 session the bill, in spite of strong opposition from the Eisenhower administration, won the support of the House Republican Policy Committee, which formally endorsed the measure on June 9. The bill then passed the House on June 24 by the relatively narrow margin of 225 to 192. Favoring the bill were 114 Republicans and 111 Democrats, practically all of the latter being southerners. The opposition came from 30 Republicans and 162 Democrats.

The language of section 1 of H. R. 3 was as follows:

No Act of Congress shall be construed as indicating an intent on the part of Congress to occupy the field in which such Act operates, to the exclusion of any State laws on the same subject matter unless such Act contains an express provision to that effect, or unless there is a direct and positive conflict between such Act and the State law so that the two cannot be reconciled or consistently stand together.

The second section of the bill, by contrast, dealt specifically with the *Nelson* problem, providing that no federal anti-subversion legislation should prevent the enforcement of state sedition statutes.

The argument for legislation with the far-reaching scope of section 1 was that the Supreme Court had used its powers to expand federal authority and to strip the states of their rightful authority, in violation of the Tenth Amendment. It was charged that *Nelson* was only one of a number of decisions in which the Court had hampered state jurisdiction by misconstruing the established rules for adjudicating federal-state controversies. The report of the House Judiciary Committee on H. R. 3 in the 1958 session sought to establish this record by referring to four decisions other than *Nelson*.

On analysis, however, it becomes evident that only one of these decisions, *Cloverleaf Co.* v. *Patterson* (1942), was relevant to the *Nelson* situation or to the proposed legislation. In *Cloverleaf* the Court, dividing five to four, concluded in an opinion by Justice Reed that the provisions of the federal Internal Revenue Code regulating the production of renovated butter precluded enforcement of an Alabama statute authorizing inspection and seizure of renovated butter determined unwholesome by state officials. The Court majority held that "where the United States exercises its power of legislation so as to conflict with a regulation of the state, either specifically or by implication, the state legislation becomes inoperative." But the opinion went on: "When the prohibition of state action is not specific but inferable from the scope and purpose of the federal legislation, it must be clear that the federal provisions are inconsistent with those of the state to justify the thwarting of state regulation."

This position was attacked by Chief Justice Stone who, speaking for the four dissenters, wrote:

The decision of the Court appears to me to depart radically from the salutary principle that Congress, in enacting legislation within its constitutional authority, will not be deemed to have intended to strike down a state statute designed to protect the health and safety of the public unless the state act, in terms or in its practical administration, conflicts with the act of Congress or plainly and palpably infringes its policy. . . .

Stone contended that in the Alabama case federal authority was limited to the manufactured product, whereas the state was being blocked by the Court from seizing spoiled materials which were to be used in making the product. "Thus both the federal and the state governments were left powerless to condemn an article which is a notorious menace to health, a substantial part of which is never shipped out of the state." Justices Frankfurter, Murphy, and Byrnes joined in this dissent.

The other cases cited by the House committee report failed to give much support to the argument against the Court. One was *Slochower* v. *Board of Higher Education of New York City* (1956), in which the Court held that New York could not discharge a professor in a public college merely because he had taken the Fifth Amendment before a Senate committee. Here the conflict of state action was with a constitutional standard, and the case had nothing whatever to do with the doctrine of preemption.

Another decision cited was *Phillips Petroleum Co.* v. *Wisconsin* (1954), where the Court by a vote of five to three ruled that an independent natural gas producer, which sold gas to interstate pipeline companies, was covered by the federal regulatory provisions of the Natural Gas Act and did not fall under the statute's exemptions for the "production or gathering of natural gas." Again, there was no doctrine of preemption applied here. The problem was solely one of determining the legislative intent of Congress, and Justice Douglas, one of the dissenters, admitted that the legislative history was "not helpful."

Still another case relied on to support H. R. 3 was *Railway Employees' Department* v. *Hanson* (1956). In that decision the Court was construing language adopted by Congress in the Railway Labor Act which expressly permitted railroads and unions to make closed shop agreements "notwithstanding . . . any other statute or law . . . of any State." The justices unanimously concluded that this clear federal legislation superseded the "right to work" provision of the Nebraska constitution. No doctrine of preemption was required here. All the Court had to do was to determine whether the statute was within the constitutional power of Congress. If it was — and the Court so held — the conflict with the state policy was direct and complete.

Though not mentioned in the House committee report, there was another Court decision, dating from 1941, which figured in congressional discussions. This was *Hines* v. *Davidowitz,* already noted as a primary reliance of the Court in the *Nelson* decision. In *Hines* the

Court held a state alien registration law to be superseded by the Federal Alien Registration Act of 1940. The Court majority thought that "the treatment of aliens, in whatever state they may be located, [was] a matter of national moment." This view was contradicted by a three-judge minority of Stone, Hughes, and McReynolds, who complained that "occupying the field" was a "vague and illusory" formula with which to justify excluding a state from enforcing legislation which was admittedly within its constitutional power to enact.

The case for H. R. 3, then, had to rest on the charge that in three Supreme Court decisions — *Hines, Cloverleaf,* and *Nelson* — two of which dated back over fifteen years, the Supreme Court had misapplied the preemption doctrine. If it was only the one recent case, *Nelson*, with which the House was concerned, it could have reversed the Court's holding simply by passing section 2 of H. R. 3. In fact, Representative Lindsay of New York sought to limit the bill to the achieving of this result by proposing an amendment striking out section 1, but the House insisted on its retention.[3]

Obviously there was something more than met the eye to this claim that these three Court decisions required the adoption of a formula which the Department of Justice characterized as far-reaching and retroactive, the effect of which could not be foretold, but which seemed certain "to change the meaning of statutes conclusively interpreted many years ago, basic statutes under which millions of dollars have been invested, under which important human relationships have been fixed." Section 1, the Department's statement continued, "would attempt to apply a new rule for determining the intent of not only the present Congress or of a future Congress, but also previous Congresses whose intent is a long concluded fact not subject to change by legislative fiat."[4]

The concern of the Department of Justice was based on the fact that the broad language of the interpretative rule stated by section 1 applied to all areas where federal and state governments had concurrent powers. As Representative Celler of New York said, this "shotgun blunderbuss approach affects broad questions of interstate

[3] *Congressional Record,* June 24, 1959, pp. 10723–8 (daily ed.).
[4] *Ibid.,* vol. 104, p. 18726.

commerce, criminal law, labor relations, transportation, immigration, aviation, pure food and drug acts, agriculture, canals, roads, mines, rivers, and so on." [5]

Advocates of the bill sought in turn to show that its impact would not be so broad as pictured, and to answer the charges about the motives behind the measure. Representative Colmer of Mississippi said on June 22, 1959:

This is not a sectional bill . . . nor is there any question of minority groups involved. This is not a bill that would prevent the enactment of civil rights legislation; it is not a bill that would curb labor unions; it is not a bill that would stop the running of the railroads in interstate commerce.

As for the actual purposes of the bill, he said, "this . . . is nothing in the world but the reenactment or rather of calling attention to a part of the Constitution [the Tenth Amendment] which apparently has been neglected." [6]

These assurances sounded hollow to opponents of the bill, particularly since every effort they made to get a clear definition of the expected impact of the bill, or specifically to limit the breadth of its coverage, was defeated by the Northern Republican–Southern Democratic coalition. Representative Walter of Pennsylvania, well-known for his leadership on the Un-American Activities Committee and one of the most vociferous opponents of the Court's national security decisions, was nevertheless opposed to section 1 of H. R. 3 because, as he said, of "my inability to determine just exactly what this legislation will do and how far-reaching it is. I have yet to hear an explanation for the enactment of this legislation." [7]

One of the greatest causes of uncertainty in interpreting the bill was its apparent retroactive effect, with potential unsettlement of all past decisions of federal-state jurisdictional relations based on pre-emption doctrine. Representative Celler offered an amendment to eliminate any possible retroactive effect of the new rule by making section 1 "applicable only to acts of Congress hereafter enacted,"

[5] *Ibid.*, June 22, 1959, p. 10464 (daily ed.).
[6] *Ibid.*, pp. 10448–9.
[7] *Ibid.*, June 23, 1959, p. 10574.

and promised that he would vote for the bill if this amendment was attached to it. The backers of the bill refused to accept the Celler amendment, and it was defeated 129 to 195.[8] Representative Fulton offered an amendment to exclude five areas from the scope of section 1 — civil rights, education, labor-management relations, rural electrification, and interstate commerce carriers — but it was beaten by a vote of 53 to 146.[9]

And so the bill retained the amorphous, omnibus character which made it attractive to a variety of interests in the House. Basically it was an anti-Court bill. "The enactment of this legislation," said Representative Rogers of Colorado, "is an attempt to tell the Supreme Court of the United States how to conduct its business, and that is very bad."[10] It was also an anti–civil rights bill. Representative Celler stated: "H. R. 3 is an expression of discontent with the liberal decision [of] the Supreme Court in the Nelson case and several others safeguarding the rights of individuals."[11] Representative O'Hara of Illinois spelled out this charge in greater detail:

Everyone knows that the real issue here is civil rights. H. R. 3 is the rock. The Supreme Court of the United States is the target. . . . My colleagues from the South, gallantly fighting on the last foothold of what they know is a lost battlefield, have wrapped themselves in the brilliant robes of the dear old doctrine of Federal preemption as they battle to the last drop of devotion for the continuance of the social order in which they believe and by which they have lived. Their strategy is superb.

But they are not fooling themselves. They know that, no matter what label they give it, this is the civil rights battle of 1959 and that the strategy they are using is patterned exactly on that of the civil rights battle in the 85th Congress when trial by jury was the battle cry.[12]

But there were also economic aspects to the legislation. In fact, section 1 was far more likely to disturb established economic relationships than any other type, and the railroads requested that they

---

[8] *Ibid.*, June 24, 1959, p. 10723.
[9] *Ibid.*, p. 10736.
[10] *Ibid.*, June 22, 1959, p. 10460.
[11] *Ibid.*, p. 10464.
[12] *Ibid.*, June 23, p. 10579.

be exempted from its provisions lest many long-dead state regulations covering their activities be revived by its language. In fact, there was something in H. R. 3 for everyone, concluded Representative Vanik of Ohio, a trial judge before his election to Congress.

There is something in it for those who seek vengeance against the Supreme Court for what it said in the segregation decision of 1954. There is something in it for those who seek to exercise States rights to protect unfortunate citizens from the civil rights they now have. There is something in this bill for those members of the law who thrive on lusty fees made by conflict of laws. There is something in this bill for some business interests who expect to reap a bonanza of profit through the deterioration and atrophy of the Federal regulatory power. There is something in this bill for practically everyone except the people of America who may never comprehend what it will do to them.[13]

As a final judgment on H. R. 3, it seems not unfair to pair the comments of Democratic Representative Celler and Republican Attorney General Rogers. Said Celler:

In a single sentence, section 1 of this bill would unsettle over a century of jurisprudence defining the bounds of Federal and State legislative power; it would throw uncounted economic and legal relationships into a state of chaos, it would impose heavy new burdens on Congress and on the courts, and expense, uncertainty and excessive litigation upon citizens. Its meaning is so obscure that its distinguished author will not tell us and the Attorney General of the United States confesses that he cannot tell us what it would accomplish.[14]

Said the Attorney General:

HR 3 is designed to revive certain State laws previously held unconstitutional because of their conflict with Federal statutes. It proposes to change the effect of these Federal statutes not by openly amending them but by passing a retroactive rule of interpretation to change the meaning the courts have given to the words now contained in these statutes without changing the words themselves.[15]

This was the bill which the House passed on June 24, 1959, by a

[13] *Ibid.*, June 24, p. 10721.
[14] *Congressional Record*, June 22, p. 10465 (daily ed.).
[15] *Ibid.*, vol. 104, p. 18726.

vote of 225 to 192. The 111 Democrats who voted for the bill were nearly all Southerners, and they were voting against the racial segregation decision. But what were the 114 Republicans who supported the bill (amounting to almost four fifths of all Republicans voting on the measure) voting for, or against? Perhaps Representative Jackson, a Republican of California, gave a clue when he stated: "For my part, I am frank to admit that my support of H. R. 3 is, in major part, emotional." [16]

[16] *Ibid.*, June 24, 1959, p. 10732.

7

⊓⊔⊓⊔⊓⊔⊓⊔⊓⊔⊓⊔⊓⊔⊓⊔⊓⊔⊓⊔⊓⊔⊓⊔⊓⊓

THE PASSPORT
ISSUE

THE State Department's policy of denying passports to communists or adherents to the Communist Party line was brought before the Supreme Court for consideration in the case of *Kent* v. *Dulles* (1958), and was invalidated as lacking any statutory authority. Justice Douglas reached this conclusion for the Court majority on the basis of an interpretation of both congressional action and non-action. The basic passport statute of 1856 appeared to give the Secretary of State broad discretionary power by providing: "The Secretary of State may grant and issue passports . . . under such rules as the President shall designate and prescribe." In practice, however, this discretion was long exercised, according to Douglas, within very narrow limits, and principally in deciding two issues. One was whether the applicant was in fact a citizen or a person "owing allegiance" to the United States. The other was whether the applicant was trying to escape from criminal prosecution, promoting passport fraud, or otherwise engaged in illegal conduct.

Occasionally, it is true, broader "public interest" questions were raised. After the Russian revolution, passports were generally refused to American communists until 1931. Again after World War II concern developed over travel by communists, and in 1947 the Secretary of State issued regulations requiring the denial of passports to (1) persons who were members of the Communist Party; (2) persons who had recently terminated their membership in the party under circumstances indicating that they continued to act under its discipline; (3) persons who engaged in activities which supported the communist movement under circumstances indicating that they were under the control and direction of the movement; or (4) persons going abroad to engage in activities which would advance the communist movement.

In the *Kent* case the Supreme Court had to decide whether the State Department had been authorized by Congress to adopt these regulations and to require applicants to sign non-communist affidavits. Justice Douglas argued that by the time the Passport Act was codified and re-enacted in 1926, State Department practice had "jelled" only around denial because of unlawful conduct or lack of citizenship. The 1926 enactment could be presumed to give congressional approval to passport denial for these two purposes, but the Court was not prepared to assume that Congress had impliedly sanctioned further controls.

There were two reasons why the Court felt it must be reluctant to assume congressional ratification of the State Department program. One was the fact that under the Immigration and Nationality Act of 1952 a passport is necessary to depart from or to enter the country. The second was the ruling, announced for the first time in this case, that "The right to travel is a part of the 'liberty' of which the citizen cannot be deprived without the due process of law of the Fifth Amendment." The Court took the position that, with a basic liberty at stake, administrative restrictions of that liberty could not be permitted to rest on the justification of implied congressional authorization.

Of course, there was legislation later than the 1926 Passport Act which bore on the question. There was the Internal Security Act of 1950 which denied passports to members of organizations required to register with the Attorney General. However, this statute was not yet in effect at the time of the *Kent* decision, because by 1958 no registration proceedings had been completed and the constitutionality of the act was still undecided by the Supreme Court. Then there was the Immigration and Nationality Act of 1952 which repeated the earlier discretionary authorizations over passport issuance to the Secretary. But the Court hesitated to find "in this broad generalized power an authority to trench so heavily on the rights of the citizen." Justice Douglas pointed out that a constitutional right was at stake "which we must assume Congress will be faithful to respect," and concluded:

We would be faced with important constitutional questions were we to hold that Congress . . . had given the Secretary authority to withhold passports to citizens because of their beliefs or associations. Congress has made no such provision in explicit terms; and absent one, the Secretary may not employ that standard to restrict the citizens' right of free movement.

The four-judge minority, composed of Justices Clark, Burton, Harlan, and Whittaker, thought that Congress had clearly acquiesced in or positively approved the State Department's use of passport denial for national security purposes. The majority's contention that passports had been denied in peacetime only where questions of allegiance or criminal activity were raised, was denied as "contrary to fact." The majority argument that the admittedly more restrictive wartime practices had no relevance for determining whether Congress intended to approve these practices by its 1952 legislation was denied as "contrary . . . to common sense."

The fact was, said Justice Clark for the minority, that the Secretary's discretionary power had long been exercised, and Congress had never sought to impose any limitations on his authority in its numerous reviews of the problem. The act of 1918, which made a passport necessary in order to enter or leave the United States during wartime, and the act of 1941, which extended this requirement during presidentially proclaimed peacetime emergencies, were incorporated into the act of 1952 practically without legislative comment. By such action, the minority believed,

Congress . . . approved whatever use of his discretion the Secretary had made prior to the June 1952 date of that legislation. That conclusion necessarily follows from the fact that [the act of 1952] continued to make legal exit or entry turn on possession of a passport, without in any way limiting the discretionary passport power theretofore exercised by the Secretary.

What appraisal can be drawn of this contrariety of views about congressional intention? The majority position was certainly somewhat tenuous in holding that Congress had ratified the Secretary's practice of denying passports which would further criminal activity but had not ratified his practice of denial on grounds of danger to national security. Whether the facts support such a distinction may be questioned, as the minority did. But the majority was on sounder ground in refusing to permit a basic right to be infringed by statutory implication. The *Kent* decision asserted for the first time the constitutional status of the right to travel as protected by the due process clause. If this right was to be limited, the majority insisted that a clear and specific statutory foundation be laid for the limitation, and that the delegation of such restrictive powers to the Secretary of State must meet the classic tests for valid legislative delegation. Even should such delegation be provided for by statute, Douglas' opinion warned that the delegation would be narrowly construed by the courts. In fact, the Court majority made clear that a real constitutional question would be raised by any legislation attempting to "curtail or dilute" the right to travel. It was no doubt largely to avoid this constitutional question that the Court majority decided the case on grounds of statutory construction and intent.

In summary, then, the majority decision in the *Kent* case can be defended on the ground that in two respects it sought to minimize the Court's legislative role. It refused to read legislative intent into a combination of administrative practice and legislative silence. Douglas said, in effect, let Congress speak for itself if it wishes to approve the State Department's practice; the Court will not speak for it. Second, the Court followed its long-standing rule of avoiding a challenge to the constitutional authority of Congress so long as any non-constitutional ground was available for deciding the case.

Passport Action in Congress

As a result of the *Kent* decision, the State Department issued passports to several known communists or communist sympathizers, who had previously been denied permission to leave the country, perhaps the best-known case being that of the singer Paul Robeson. These actions were given widespread publicity as creating a serious security situation, and both the State Department and President Eisenhower forwarded urgent pleas to Congress to adopt legislation restoring the Department's discretionary power over the issuance of passports. The Department asked for blanket authority to deny passports to any person for any reason related to foreign policy. It also requested the right to use confidential information in reaching a decision to deny, thus refusing to make any accommodation to the serious criticisms that had been leveled at this practice in the past.

The failure of Congress even to consider a passport bill of the type requested by the administration at the close of the 1958 session has already been noted. Instead the House produced a much less restrictive bill, with a substantial amount of procedural protection for passport applicants against adverse State Department action. For example, the bill provided, in section 8: "No application for a passport may be denied under . . . this act except after opportunity for a hearing. A denial of a passport pursuant to . . . this act shall be subject to judicial review in the district courts of the United States." However, even this milder measure failed to secure Senate consideration.

In the 86th Congress the House Foreign Affairs Committee produced another bill along the same comparatively moderate lines, and the House passed it on September 8, 1959, by a vote of 371 to 18.[1] Because of its importance, the provisions of the bill should be noted in somewhat more detail. The bill began with a finding that the international communist movement is hostile to the United States; that travel by couriers and agents is a major and essential means by which the international communist movement is promoted; and that consequently issuance of passports should be denied to supporters of the movement for use to promote the purposes of the movement.

Before the Secretary of State could deny a passport, however, the bill required him to make two findings: first, that the applicant is or

[1] H. R. 9069, 86th Cong.; *Congressional Record*, pp. 17079–80 (daily ed.).

had been, since January 1, 1951, a member of, or affiliated with, the Communist Party, or knowingly engaged since the same date in activities intended to further the international communist movement; second, that the person's activities or presence abroad would be harmful to the security of the United States. These provisions were purposely drafted to prevent the government from denying passports to persons merely because they had once belonged to the Communist Party or any other organization. The bill as amended specifically provided: "The Secretary of State shall not deny a passport to any person solely on the basis of membership in any organization, or association with any individual or group."

The bill contained certain administrative safeguards. No application for a passport could be denied and no passport could be revoked except after opportunity for a hearing, in the judicial district in which the applicant resides. Moreover, any such denial or revocation would be subject to judicial review "on the record" in the federal district courts. There was considerable disagreement as to the meaning of the phrase, "on the record," which was said by Representative Bentley to be the "most controversial language in the entire bill," [2] and an amendment was offered to strike it from the measure. The State Department opposed this language on the ground that it would require revealing in court confidential information and perhaps also the sources of that information. Representative Hays replied that it was "serious business" to deny a person a passport, and that if it was done wrongfully there must be redress in the courts. The only way to establish whether the action was wrongful was to have a court review the grounds for the administrative decision. If the State Department "cannot submit the data on which they relied to support their decision, they can just issue the passport," Rep. Hays concluded.[3]

In spite of the overwhelming vote by which the passport bill passed the House in 1959, it was never reported out of the Senate Foreign Relations Committee. That committee considered three Senate-sponsored proposals. One bill, presented by Senator Wiley of Wis-

[2] *Ibid.*, p. 17069.
[3] *Ibid.*, p. 17070.

consin, spelled out the administration's views. Robert Murphy, Deputy Under Secretary of State, contended that the State Department did not want authority to deny passports because of a person's "associations or beliefs," but only because of an applicant's activities in advancing the communist movement. "We do believe," he said, "that present membership in the Communist party, or present activities under party discipline or under the direction of the Communist movement, regardless of any formal affiliation with the Communist party, should be considered as activities in furtherance of the international Communist movement." An applicant who fell in such a category should be required to assume the burden of proof that he would not engage in pro-communist activities abroad. The Secretary should not have to demonstrate the specific harm the applicant might do on a specific future trip.

Senator Fulbright, chairman of the committee, had introduced a measure somewhat less stringent than that of Senator Wiley, and he criticized the State Department for its record on the passport question. Before the *Kent* decision, he said, the Department had been "defensive and uncooperative," and since the decision, it had taken a year for the Department to appear before his committee with recommendations. Mr. Murphy stated the Department's objection to the Fulbright bill as severely restrictive of the Secretary's existing authority "to act on considerations of foreign policy in the passport field." There was also before the committee a very liberal bill introduced by Senator Hubert Humphrey which in general would have prevented the Secretary of State from denying passports to anyone except in time of war or where the applicant was charged with, or under sentence for, a felony.[4] None of these bills was reported out of the Senate committee.

Area Travel Restrictions

Thus the congressional efforts to fill the vacuum left by the Court's decision failed in both the 1958 and 1959 sessions. In the meantime, the court of appeals for the District of Columbia came to the support of the State Department's right to deny passports to Ameri-

[4] *The New York Times,* July 14, 1959.

cans for travel to Red China and other communist nations with which this country does not maintain diplomatic relations. The Department had taken up the passport of William Worthy, a newspaperman, after he had traveled to Red China in 1956 in violation of the State Department's ban.

In 1958 the Department amended its policy to grant certain newsmen permission to go to China, but Worthy's request for a new passport was denied. He brought court action to compel the Department to give him a passport, but a three-judge panel of the court of appeals ruled unanimously in June, 1959, that area restrictions were a matter of foreign policy beyond the control of the courts. The *Kent* case was distinguished on the ground that the denial of a passport to Worthy was based in no way on "beliefs, associations or personal characteristics." Rather it was a non-discriminatory policy resting on the conclusion of the executive branch that it can protect the national interest and perhaps prevent a war by limiting the right to travel, not only of persons representing the press, but of any citizens who might wish to take risks in troubled areas of the world.[5]

One month after the *Worthy* decision, the same court rejected the claim of Waldo Frank, author and lecturer, who contended that the State Department's refusal to grant him a passport good in Red China was discriminatory in view of the fact that forty other newsmen had been given such authorizations. The judicial view was that the State Department's decision in this matter was "political in the highest sense and is not reviewable on any basis in any circumstance by any court."[6]

On December 7, 1959, the Supreme Court occasioned considerable surprise by refusing to review these decisions on certiorari, and also a similar ruling against Rep. Charles O. Porter, Democrat of Oregon, who had asked the State Department in the preceding June for permission to visit Red China to study trade possibilities and other matters. Rep. Porter contended that the State Department ban was preventing members of Congress from securing the information necessary to the making of wise legislative decisions.[7] When the

[5] 270 F.2d 905.
[6] 269 F.2d 245.   [7] 80 S. Ct. 255, 256, 260.

Supreme Court's denial of certiorari was handed down, Justice Douglas noted that he had not participated in the consideration of the Worthy or Frank petitions, presumably because he himself had previously requested permission to visit China and had been refused by the State Department.

In all three cases where Supreme Court review was sought, counsel for the applicants had relied heavily on the decision in the *Kent* case, contending that the Court ruling meant that legislative authorization was needed for all travel restrictions, and that Congress had not given it. By refusing to discuss this issue, the Supreme Court left unchallenged the government's authority to forbid all travel to certain countries at its discretion. In addition to Communist China, several other countries, including Bulgaria, Albania, and Outer Mongolia, had been closed to travel by Americans.

The 1959 House passport bill, it should be noted, included provisions giving explicit statutory support for the area travel ban policy. Title II of the proposed legislation would have authorized the President to prohibit travel — with any exceptions he wished to make for specific individuals — to countries at war with the United States, countries where armed hostilities are in progress, and countries where the President finds that travel must be restricted in the national interest either because the government is unable to provide adequate protection to citizens traveling therein, or because such travel would seriously impair the foreign relations of the United States. The President's area limitations were required to be established by annual declaration, and the bill also provided that specific reasons for the limitations had to be stated annually and in detail by executive order.

As already noted, the Senate took no action on the House passport bill, H. R. 9069, during the 1959 session. However, on June 30, 1960, the Senate Judiciary Committee suddenly reported out an omnibus internal security bill, S. 2652, sponsored by Senators Thomas J. Dodd and Kenneth Keating, which had an extended passport section. The Dodd-Keating proposal was in fact a much more stringent measure than the House had passed, particularly in providing for the denial of passports on the basis of confidential information and for exclusive administrative passport review procedure within the State Department.

The Senate bill, however, had no chance of adoption, or even of consideration, in 1960. Senator Fulbright, chairman of the Senate Foreign Relations Committee, served notice that if the bill came up he would move for its referral to his committee, since it was mainly passport legislation. In any case the Senate had shown no previous disposition to accept this kind of restrictive passport control measure.

The passport problem was thus passed on to the 1961 session of Congress. It seems reasonable to assume that eventually Congress will respond to the *Kent* decision by passing a law specifically stating the powers of the Secretary of State over the issuance of passports. If that legislation is essentially the same as the bill passed by the House in 1958 and 1959, it will constitute a long step toward bringing the State Department's discretion under a reasonable measure of control. It will also constitute justification for the position of the Court majority in *Kent*, when they refused to assume that Congress had intended, by vague statutory language and by inaction, to approve the State Department's arbitrary exercise of passport powers. For, once Congress was required to address its attention to the passport issue by the *Kent* decision, it began to appear that there was strong legislative support for restrictions on the power to deny passports, and for judicial review over the administrative processes of the State Department. This is a far different picture of "legislative intent" than was argued by the Court minority in *Kent*.

8

⎍⎍⎍⎍⎍⎍⎍⎍⎍⎍⎍⎍⎍⎍⎍⎍⎍⎍⎍⎍⎍⎍⎍

THE LOYALTY-SECURITY ISSUE

ONE of the earliest results of the Cold War was the institution of a program for checking the loyalty and reliability of government employees and other workers in jobs where national security was involved. President Truman set up an elaborate procedure for reviewing employees' loyalty in 1947, and President Eisenhower continued it in a somewhat revised form in 1953. All federal employees and applicants for employment were required to undergo a loyalty check, in which the FBI assisted in an investigative role. The Department of Justice prepared a list of subversive organizations to help guide the decisions of loyalty boards of various agencies. Hearings were held by these boards when damaging information was received about an employee or applicant, but some of the customary protections of the hearing procedure – particularly the right to be informed of the source of the charges and to confront the persons making the accusation – were not guaranteed in these proceedings.

In addition to the general federal program, there were the separate security programs operated by the Atomic Energy Commission, covering perhaps one hundred fifty thousand employees at any one time, and by the armed services. Moreover, there was a procedure for scrutinizing seamen and waterfront workers, who needed port security cards in order to hold their jobs, and an industrial security pro-

96

gram which covered some three million defense plant workers operating in industries with access to secret or classified material.

The Earlier Decisions

The Supreme Court first gave attention to the serious constitutional questions posed by this staggering system of surveillance, applying to perhaps thirteen million positions in government and private industry, in two 1951 decisions. In *Joint Anti-Fascist Refugee Committee* v. *McGrath*, the Court condemned the absence of procedural protections in the listing of "subversive organizations" by the Attorney General. The second case, *Bailey* v. *Richardson*, saw the Court divided four to four on the basic issue whether the hearings accorded in loyalty proceedings met due process standards.

Subsequently the Warren Court decided three cases covering aspects of the loyalty-security program between 1955 and 1957, but in none did it come to grips with the constitutional issues. *Peters* v. *Hobby* (1955) had to do with a professor of medicine at Yale University who was employed part time as a consultant to the United States Public Health Service in work not sensitive or confidential, and giving him no access to classified material. Under the procedure provided by President Truman's executive order setting up the loyalty system, Peters was twice cleared by agency loyalty boards. The executive order also set up a central loyalty review board with reviewing authority over the decisions of the agency boards. This central body ordered a post-audit of Dr. Peters' case four years after the original charges had been met successfully. As a result of this review, the board determined that Peters must be discharged on loyalty grounds and be barred from the federal service for three years. The Supreme Court reversed this order by a vote of six to three, because it found that the board's procedure in handling the case violated the President's executive order.

Cole v. *Young* (1956) was a case involving a food inspector and preference-eligible veteran employed by the Food and Drug Administration in New York. He was investigated under the provisions of President Eisenhower's executive order, which had superseded the Truman order and made some changes in the system. Cole was

97

charged with close association with communists and with attending meetings of organizations on the Attorney General's list. He refused on principle to explain the charges against him, and the Secretary of Health, Education, and Welfare ordered his dismissal. Cole then asked for a re-opening of the case, in order to prove that his associations were innocent, but this was denied. He appealed to the Civil Service Commission under the terms of the Veterans' Preference Act of 1944, but the Commission ruled that the right of appeal provided to veterans by this act had been eliminated by the Summary Suspension Act of 1950 giving department heads certain summary suspension and unreviewable dismissal powers.[1] By a six to three vote the Supreme Court reversed that interpretation.

The third case was *Service* v. *Dulles* (1957). Service, a career officer of the Foreign Service, was arrested in 1945 on the charge that he had furnished copies of his official reports to the editor of *Amerasia* magazine. When the grand jury failed to indict him, he was restored to duty. Between 1945 and 1951 he was subjected to no fewer than six inquiries by the State Department loyalty board, and was cleared each time. The last three of these clearances were post-audited by the central loyalty review board. Twice it remanded the case to the Department for further consideration, and the third time it decided to conduct a hearing itself, as a result of which it advised the Department that Service should be removed from office.

Secretary of State Acheson acted on this advisory recommendation in December, 1951. Service having been kept dangling for six years while his reliability was being questioned, another six years were required for a final judicial decision to be reached on this administrative action. In 1957 the Supreme Court unanimously (Justice Clark not participating) reversed the ouster and restored Service to his position, contending that the State Department had not followed its own regulations in handling the case.

Avoiding Constitutional Questions

Thus in all three cases the Court reversed loyalty ousters without passing on any of the serious constitutional issues inherent in the

[1] 64 Stat. 476.

federal program. The decisions were reached rather on the basis of construction and interpretation of statutes and executive orders. The Court took this course in spite of the efforts of petitioners' counsel in all cases to get rulings against the program on constitutional grounds. Thurman Arnold, counsel for Peters, in his brief had not questioned the authority of the loyalty review board to post-audit agency board decisions. When Justice Harlan asked him about the Board's authority to conduct a post-audit, he replied: "Frankly, your Honor, I had not anticipated that problem." He went on to say that he would not like to win the case on that ground, but Justice Frankfurter cut in: "The question is not whether you want to win the case on that ground or not. This Court reaches constitutional issues last, not first." [2]

So the Court decided the *Peters* case on the ground that the post-audit was patently in violation of the President's executive order. The order was construed by the Court, speaking through Chief Justice Warren, to limit the Board's jurisdiction to appeals from adverse rulings, whereas the regulations issued by the Board under the order asserted authority over appeals from favorable rulings as well. Likewise the regulations permitted the board to adjudicate cases on its own motion, whereas the order was construed by the Chief Justice to permit referral to the board only on the motion of the employee or his agency.

In the *Cole* case the Court avoided constitutional problems by concentrating upon the interrelation of two acts of Congress. The Veterans' Preference Act of 1944 guaranteed veterans the right to appeal to the Civil Service Commission against removal from government employment. But the Summary Suspension Act of 1950 had conferred unreviewable dismissal powers on the heads of eleven named departments where it was deemed necessary or advisable in the interest of national security, and had authorized the President to extend the provisions of the act to other departments. President Eisenhower's executive order had taken advantage of this authorization to extend the summary dismissal power to all other departments and agencies of the government, and the Secretary of the Depart-

[2] *New York Times*, April 29, 1955.

ment of Health, Education, and Welfare had acted under this authority.

Cole's dismissal without appeal to the Civil Service Commission was admittedly invalid if the Veterans' Preference Act was still in effect, and the Court majority thought it was. The 1950 statute, said Justice Harlan for the Court, related only to activities directly concerned with the nation's safety as distinguished from the general welfare. In referring to "national security" Congress meant to cover "only those activities of the Government that are directly concerned with the protection of the Nation from internal subversion or foreign oppression." Congress had enumerated eleven of these "sensitive" agencies in the statute, and had left it to the President to designate others. If the Secretary of Health, Education, and Welfare was going to exercise the authority of summary dismissal provided by the 1950 act, the position must be proved to be a sensitive one. Since no such proof had been offered, the protection of the regular dismissal procedures for veterans remained in effect, the Court concluded.

In the *Service* case the controlling question as the Court saw it was the effect of the so-called McCarran rider which was annually attached to the State Department's appropriation act from 1947 on. It gave the Secretary "absolute discretion" to fire any officer or employee whenever he deemed it necessary or advisable in the interests of the United States. The Secretary, however, had not chosen to interpret this language as completely eliminating the need for procedural limitations in handling loyalty-security removals. In a 1950 report to the Senate Foreign Relations Committee the Department said that it did not believe Congress had intended to "countenance the use of 'Gestapo' methods or harassment or persecution of loyal employees . . . on flimsy evidence or hearsay or innuendo." Consequently, the Department reported that it had "proceeded to develop appropriate procedures designed to implement fully and properly the authority granted the Department under the McCarran rider." Later in 1950 President Truman wrote to the Secretary of State and, referring specifically to the annual McCarran rider just adopted by Congress, reminded the Secretary of the necessity "to protect the national security without unduly jeopardizing the personal liberties of . . . employees," and instructed the State Department to abide by the procedural requirements of the Summary Suspension Act of 1950.

The Court unanimously concluded that the Secretary had consciously decided to impose upon his Department "more rigorous substantive and procedural standards" than the McCarran rider would have required. He was not obligated to adopt this course, but neither was he forbidden "to bind himself by these Regulations as to McCarran Rider discharges." Congress had been advised that the Secretary had seen fit to limit by regulations the discretion conferred upon him, but it had continued to re-enact the rider without change in several succeeding years. Such congressional inaction, the Court inferred, ratified the Secretary's interpretation of the rider. Consequently, the Court held that the regulations were valid. The Department had purported to conduct the Service discharge proceedings under these regulations, but the Court found that the regulations had actually not been observed in some respects. So the discharge was invalid.

In two of these three decisions a judicial minority disputed the reasoning and the conclusions of the Court. In the *Peters* case Justices Douglas, Reed, and Burton charged the Court with making a too literal interpretation of the executive order and with refusing to give proper weight to consistent administrative practice which contradicted the Court's interpretation.[3] The dissenters noted that the regulation which the Court was holding illegal in 1955 had been adopted in 1947. Every year from 1948 through 1952 the results of the Board's post-audit actions were reported in the annual reports of the Civil Service Commission, which were submitted to the President under statutory requirement. These reports also clearly showed that the Board was rehearing cases on its own motion. The President had allowed these practices to continue, after having been officially informed of them. "Such reasonable interpretation promptly adopted and long-continued by the President and the Board should be re-

---

[3] Justice Douglas did not agree with Reed and Burton in disposing of the case, however. While he agreed that the Board's procedures were justified under the executive order, he would have declared the executive order unconstitutional. Justices Reed and Burton did not reach the constitutional issue.

spected by the courts," wrote Justice Reed. Presidential orders and rules made thereunder, he added, should not be subjected to the same degree of judicial review as would be applied to congressional legislation, because the executive branch "is traditionally free to handle its internal problems of administration in its own way."

In the *Cole* case the dissenters thought that the limitations which the Court majority found in the Summary Suspension Act of 1950 were based on "a chain of inferences." The Court's opinion, Justice Clark charged, frustrated "the clear purpose of the Congress" in adopting the act. Section 3 of the statute, which contained the presidential authorization, had no limiting words whatever, yet the Court concluded that the President was limited by the section to dealing with "sensitive" employees. Such an interpretation intruded the Court "into presidential policy making," and substituted judicial for executive judgment. Moreover, Clark contended that Congress had ratified the presidential interpretation because it had been discussed in both houses and appropriations had been made in subsequent years for investigations under its provisions without any question's being raised.

As for the Court's announced purpose of avoiding constitutional questions, Clark argued that the *Cole* decision had raised, and failed to settle, a serious issue about the President's power to remove executive employees whose further employment he believed to be inconsistent with the national security. This power might rest directly on Article II of the Constitution and not on any grant of authority from Congress, Clark noted, and the issue should be faced in any opinion holding an executive order inoperative, but the majority had failed to do so.

Congressional Action

These three initial decisions of the Warren Court thus left the important constitutional questions raised by the federal loyalty-security program undetermined. The principal practical effect resulted from the *Cole* decision limiting security procedures to "sensitive" positions — perhaps five hundred thousand out of the total federal civilian personnel. Bills were introduced in both the 1958 and 1959 sessions of Congress restoring full coverage to the security system; the provisions were that all employees of any department or agency of the government were deemed to be employed in an activity involving national security. This legislation was proposed in spite of the fact that all the responsible studies of the federal loyalty-security system had concluded that it was utterly futile and terribly costly in money and manpower to put every mail carrier and federal building janitor through the security machinery.[4]

As already noted, the *Cole* repealer [5] came within a hair's breadth of passage at the close of the 1958 session. The elaborate report of a Special Commission on Government Security, headed by Loyd Wright, had been presented to Congress in June, 1957, and the expectation had been that this report would provide a basis for a statutory revamping of the entire federal security program. The report did make certain drastic recommendations for revision of the system, but it was disappointing to those who had hoped that it would correct some of its harshness and procedural defects. On the issue of coverage, the Wright report, rather than proposing a limitation to sensitive positions, thought the loyalty system should be extended from the executive to the legislative and judicial branches of the government and even to employees of the civil air transport companies.

It soon became apparent that no over-all legislative revisions of the security system could be adopted during the 1958 term, so bills limited to reversal of the *Cole* rule were passed in both houses. As agreed to in conference committee, the measure was to be effective only until June 30, 1959, by which time, it was assumed, a general statute based on the Wright report would have been adopted. The conference report was accepted in the House on August 22, but lack of enthusiasm on the part of the managers of the bill for the Senate led them to let it die by default in the closing hours of the 85th Congress.

[4] See Ralph S. Brown, Jr., *Loyalty and Security: Employment Tests in the United States* (Yale University Press, 1958); Eleanor Bontecue, *The Federal Loyalty-Security Program* (Cornell University Press, 1953); Dudley B. Bonsal, *The Federal Loyalty-Security Program* (Dodd, Mead, 1956).
[5] S. 1411, 85th Cong.

The 1959 Decisions

On June 29, 1959, the Supreme Court returned to the loyalty-security problem in three additional cases, only one of which was of major significance. In *Taylor* v. *McElroy* the suit was held moot because the employee had been cleared and restored to his job after the Supreme Court agreed to hear the case. *Vitarelli* v. *Seaton* concerned a non–civil service employee of the Department of the Interior who, although the Department could have summarily discharged him without cause, was in fact put through a security procedure and discharged on security grounds. The Court ruled that the government, having once invoked the security procedures, had to follow them, and since it had not done so Vitarelli was ordered restored to his position.

The most important of these three decisions, *Greene* v. *McElroy*, concerned the industrial security program in effect for private plants doing work for the government involving access to classified or secret information. Greene, an aeronautical engineer earning $18,000 a year, was denied security clearance by the Navy, and since his firm had no unclassified projects on which he could work, he was discharged. He was accused of past association with communists, but as was customary in security hearings, he was not informed of the source of the charges against him or permitted to confront his accusers.

The Supreme Court, with only Justice Clark dissenting, ruled that a hearing of this type "failed to comport with our traditional ideas of fair procedure." Chief Justice Warren thought it was a "relatively immutable" principle of our jurisprudence that "where governmental action seriously injures an individual, and the reasonableness of the action depends on fact findings, the evidence used to prove the Government's case must be disclosed to the individual so that he has an opportunity to show that it is untrue." The Court avoided a direct holding of unconstitutionality of the industrial security program, however, by deciding that neither the President nor Congress had authorized security procedures which dispensed with the confrontation safeguard.

While the Court thus once more avoided a constitutional attack on the security program, Chief Justice Warren's intimations of unconstitutionality of the procedures followed were so clear and plain that three justices—Frankfurter, Harlan, and Whittaker—wrote concurring opinions disassociating themselves from any views about the validity of the government's procedures. Justice Harlan also used his concurring opinion for a rather unusual rebuke to Justice Clark who, as the sole dissenter, had misrepresented the majority ruling in an inexcusable fashion. Harlan wrote:

It is regrettable that my brother Clark should have so far yielded to the temptations of colorful characterization as to depict the issue in this case as being whether a citizen has "a constitutional right to have access to the Government's military secrets," and to suggest that the Court's action today requires "the President's Cabinet members to revoke their refusal to give" the petitioner "access to military secrets," despite any views they may have as to his reliability. Of course this decision involves no such issue or consequences.

If an industrial security system was to be continued after the *Greene* decision, it was mandatory either for Congress to enact legislation authorizing such a system without procedural protections — legislation which would then have to run the Supreme Court gantlet of constitutionality — or for the President to adopt a new system which would give appropriate recognition to the Supreme Court's concerns about opportunities for confrontation and cross-examination.

Representative Walter sought to follow the former course, and he prepared a bill permitting the Defense Department to make security risk findings without confrontation and cross-examination. His bill provided that any industrial security procedures set up by the Secretary of Defense "shall be designed to protect from disclosure all information which, in the opinion of the Secretary, would affect the national security, safety, or public interest, or would tend to compromise investigative sources or investigative methods." This controversial bill slipped through the House on February 2, 1960 by adoption on the consent calendar when its opponents failed to realize what was happening.[6]

[6] H. R. 8121; *Congressional Record*, pp. 1628–9 (daily ed.).

Adoption by the Senate would have been most unlikely, but the matter was taken out of legislative hands on February 20 when President Eisenhower issued a long-awaited executive order setting up a new industrial security program which took account of the Supreme Court's objections as expressed in the *Greene* case. The order significantly enlarged the right of accused security risks to confront and cross-examine their accusers. It made confrontation the general rule, though with some specific exceptions. The principal loophole provided was for any "confidential informant who has been engaged in obtaining intelligence information for the Government." In such cases the head of the department or investigative agency furnishing his secret statement would have to certify that "disclosure of his identity would be substantially harmful to the national interest." But where complete confrontation was denied, the accused person had to be given a summary of the informant's statement, as "detailed as the national security permits"; the fact that the accused was not allowed to cross-examine the informant would have to be taken into account by those deciding the case; and a final decision adverse to the accused could be made only by the head of the department — the Secretary of Defense in most cases — "upon his personal review of the case." The order also required any final decision denying or revoking clearance to show the reasons for the decision. Though experience alone will determine how these exceptions are to be interpreted in practice, it is clear that the *Greene* decision was directly responsible for significant improvements in the procedural protections accorded in the industrial security program.

9

╓╙╜╓╙╜╓╙╜╓╙╜╓╙╜╓╙╜╓╙╜╓╙╜╓╙╜╓╙╜╓╙╜

STATE LIMITATIONS ON
EMPLOYMENT

SOME of the bitterest attacks on the Warren Court were occasioned by two decisions rendered in 1957, dealing with admission to the practice of law in the states. In both cases the Supreme Court reversed state action and ordered admission to the bar for applicants who had been rejected by the state procedures. One of the cases, *Konigsberg* v. *State Bar of California*, was characterized by the Conference of Chief Justices of the states in their 1958 report as reaching "the high water mark so far established by the Supreme Court in overthrowing the action of a state and in denying to a state the power to keep order in its own house."

Communist Party Membership

Decisions in the two cases turned on somewhat different considerations, and they belong to somewhat different lines of constitutional development. The case of *Schware* v. *New Mexico Board of Bar Examiners* had to do with an applicant who had been denied admission to the bar because he did not meet the requirement of "good moral character." The grounds were, first, that between 1934 and 1937 he had used certain aliases. His explanation was that they were adopted so he could secure employment in businesses which discriminated against Jews and organize non-Jewish employees more effectively. Second, he had been arrested several times during this period in the course of labor disputes and recruiting for the Spanish Loyalists, but in each instance he had been released and no charges had been filed. The most important charge was that he was an admitted member of the Communist Party from 1932 to 1940, and this was the fact on which the state authorities relied most heavily in disqualifying him.

The Supreme Court had in previous opinions adopted the position that current membership in the Communist Party was a relevant consideration in determining qualification for public employment. *Garner* v. *Board of Public Works* (1951) had upheld a Los Angeles requirement of a non-communist affidavit from its employees, Justice Frankfurter saying: "In the context of our time, such membership is sufficiently relevant to effective and dependable government, and to the confidence of the electorate in its government."

This general position was repeated in *Gerende* v. *Board of Supervisors* (1951) involving affidavits for candidates for elective office, and *Adler* v. *Board of Education of City of New York* (1952), which grew out of a statutory plan to bar schoolteachers who belonged to organizations advocating the overthrow of government by unlawful means. But in *Wieman* v. *Updegraff* (1952) the Court unanimously invalidated a state oath requirement for public employees because it failed to distinguish between innocent and knowing membership in organizations with illegal purposes. Justice Clark wrote in that opinion: "Indiscriminate classification of innocent with knowing activity must fall as an assertion of arbitrary power. The oath offends due process."

The *Schware* case presented two new problems. It involved past, not current, membership in the Communist Party, and it was not public employment but publicly licensed private employment that was at stake. This is not the place to review at length the development of judicial attitudes toward state occupational licensing requirements. The right to earn one's livelihood "by any lawful calling" was recognized by the Supreme Court in *Allgeyer* v. *Louisiana* (1897), but occupational licensing to protect the public health, morals, and safety against "unfit" practitioners of important public callings or "unfair practices" has always been recognized as justified.

Legislative regulations of occupations have generally been presumed to be justified by the public interest, and they have seldom been judicially nullified, though in fact the motivation of much occupational licensing has been to protect those already in the field from too much competition.[1] The network of state occupational requirements which has grown up is so restrictive that, as Roger Cramton has said: "Many young Americans who can aspire to be President of the United States must resign themselves to the fact that they cannot become barbers, carpenters, chiropodists, electricians, funeral directors, hypertrichologists, pharmacists, photographers, plumbers, and veterinarians, among others."[2]

In spite of its permissiveness about state regulation of occupations, the Supreme Court has never abandoned its position that freedom of occupational choice is protected by the due process clause. Barriers to entrance into a profession must have some rational relation to fitness for the profession. In the *Schware* case the Court found no such relation. A majority of the justices, speaking through Justice Black, reviewed the adverse conclusions of the examiners on all the grounds raised, independently reassessed the facts, and concluded that there was no basis in the evidence for inferences of bad moral character.

Three justices — Frankfurter, Clark, and Harlan — confined their reversal of state action to the issue of former Communist Party membership, and since this is the aspect of the case on which the entire Court was united, the Frankfurter opinion is particularly important. He concentrated on this statement by the New Mexico supreme court: "We believe one who has knowingly given his loyalties to such a program and belief for six or seven years during a period of responsible adulthood is a person of questionable character." Frankfurter regarded this as a conclusion of law "so dogmatic . . . as to be wholly unwarranted," and went on:

History overwhelmingly establishes that many youths like the peti-

---

[1] See, for example, *Kotch* v. *Board of River Port Pilot Commissioners* (1947).

[2] "Supercession and Subversion: Limitations on State Power to Deal with Issues of Subversion and Loyalty," *University of Chicago Law School Record*, vol. 8 (1958), p. 42.

tioner were drawn by the mirage of communism during the depression era, only to have their eyes later opened to reality. Such experiences no doubt may disclose a woolly mind or naive notions regarding the problems of society. But facts of history that we would be arbitrary in rejecting bar the presumption, let alone an irrebuttable presumption, that response to foolish, baseless hopes regarding the betterment of society made those who had entertained them but who later undoubtedly came to their senses and their sense of responsibility "questionable characters." Since the Supreme Court of New Mexico as a matter of law took a contrary view of such a situation in denying petitioner's application, it denied him due process of law.

In other words, denial of admission to the bar because of an irrebuttable presumption that past membership in the Communist Party establishes bad moral character was unjustified and contrary to due process.

The Right of Silence

Konigsberg v. *State Bar of California*, though also a bar admission case, presented a quite different situation. The Court was not unanimous, and the constitutional issue was related to the larger question of the right to silence before official investigatory bodies. Prior to *Konigsberg*, the Court had expressed itself on this matter, though not with too much consistency. In the case of *In re Anastaplo* (1955) an applicant for the Illinois bar who had refused on the basis of the First Amendment to answer the examiners' questions about his political beliefs and was consequently denied admission, could not get the Supreme Court to accept his case on certiorari.

But in *Slochower* v. *Board of Higher Education of New York City* (1956) the Court did act favorably in upholding the right of silence. A professor at Brooklyn College had been fired because he refused under the Fifth Amendment to testify before a Senate committee as to his political associations before 1941. The New York City charter provided for the automatic firing of any employee who used the privilege against self-incrimination to avoid answering a question relating to his official conduct. By a five to four vote the Court annulled the dismissal on the ground that the charter provision converted the employee's claim of privilege "into a conclusive presumption of guilt," whereas no inference of guilt was permissible from a Fifth Amendment claim.

The *Konigsberg* case involved a bar applicant who, like Anastaplo, had declined to answer questions about his political beliefs. There was some disagreement on the Court as to whether the examiners had barred him because of his non-cooperation, or because of negative findings about his character and loyalty. A five-judge majority adopted the latter explanation, and reversed the board's conclusion as contrary to the evidence. Konigsberg's career in social work, his military service, and his law school record had all been exemplary. His character references were overwhelmingly favorable. One ex-communist testified that Konigsberg had attended meetings of a communist unit in 1941, though the witness did not claim to know him personally and the identification was not too convincing. In 1950 Konigsberg had written newspaper articles criticizing the Korean war, big business, racial discrimination, and certain Supreme Court decisions, but Justice Black could not see how this indicated "bad moral character."

Justice Frankfurter, dissenting, would have remanded the case to the state court for certification of the grounds for its declination to review, but Justices Harlan and Clark attacked the premises of the majority decision directly. Justice Black had sought to offset the effect of Konigsberg's refusal to testify in several ways. He held that the California denial of his application was not based solely on this ground, in spite of the great emphasis placed on this action by the bar examiners. He found that the refusal to cooperate with the examiners by testifying to his political beliefs and affiliations was in "good faith," contrary to the implied finding of the state officials. Though recognizing the validity of the state statute that placed the burden of proof on the applicant, the majority apparently conceived that the state was obliged to produce affirmative evidence of present unsatisfactory moral character in order to deny admission to the bar.

Justice Harlan took a different view. The issue for him was not whether the record contained sufficient evidence to demonstrate as a factual matter that Konigsberg had a bad moral character. Rather, the issue was whether a state bar committee violates the Fourteenth

Amendment when it declines to certify for admission an applicant who obstructs a proper investigation into his qualifications by deliberately refusing to answer questions relevant to his fitness under valid standards, and who thus fails to carry the burden of proof to establish that he is qualified.

The *Schware* and *Konigsberg* decisions brought immediate reactions in Congress. The Jenner bill of 1957 had as one of its main purposes retaliation against the Court for these decisions. Under this bill, it will be recalled, issues pertaining to admission to the bar in any state would have been foreclosed from reaching the Supreme Court. In the 1958 revision by Senator Butler of the Jenner bill, this was the only area in which withdrawal of the Supreme Court's appellate jurisdiction was retained. When the bill was reported to the Senate on August 20, 1958, Senator Butler sought to make it more palatable by adding a proviso that it should not apply to denials of admission to practice law when a charge of "discrimination based on race, color, or religion" was involved. However, the measure was lost by a vote to lay on the table in the last week of the 1958 session.

Public Employee Removals

Even before the defeat of the Jenner-Butler bill, however, the Supreme Court seemed to suggest in two 1958 decisions that it might be abandoning the position taken in the *Konigsberg* case. *Lerner* v. *Casey* and *Beilan* v. *Board of Public Education* saw the Court upholding the dismissal of public employees who had refused to answer questions about political affiliation. Lerner was a New York subway conductor, Beilan a public schoolteacher. Lerner refused to tell New York city authorities whether he was a member of the Communist Party, and was dismissed as a person of "doubtful trust and reliability" because of his "lack of candor." Beilan refused to tell his superintendent whether he had held a certain position in the Communist Party in 1944, and later took the Fifth Amendment before a House Committee; he was dismissed for "incompetency."

The Court majority (Harlan, Burton, Frankfurter, Clark, and Whittaker) upheld the official action in both cases, contending that the employees were not removed because of a Fifth Amendment plea (as in Slochower's case), or because of their beliefs or associations, or because they were security risks, but only because their refusal to answer questions put by their employers constituted evidence of their unreliability and incompetence.

The four dissenters — Warren, Brennan, Black, and Douglas — had all been in the *Konigsberg* majority. They could not accept such "transparent denials" of the real reasons for the removals. Brennan, with Warren's concurrence, contended that each petitioner had been branded a "disloyal American" on the basis of evidence and through a procedure which could not possibly support such a finding, and so had been denied due process of law. For Black and Douglas this was another case of penalizing people for their beliefs, tracing back to the "initial error in all this business," the 1951 *Dennis* decision and its "disregard of the basic principle that government can concern itself only with the actions of men, not with their opinions or beliefs."

While it is true that the *Beilan* and *Lerner* cases may seem to cast some doubt on the continued validity of the *Konigsberg* decision, they can be distinguished from problems of admission to the bar, and in fact the authors of both decisions were careful to distinguish them from *Konigsberg*. *Beilan* and *Lerner* applied a public employees doctrine that traces back to the *Garner* and *Adler* cases. They dealt with situations where, in part because of the statutes involved, a refusal to answer questions was regarded as ipso facto disqualifying for public employment. In the situation thus created, a refusal to answer was held to constitute incompetency, and even obstruction. Warnings to this effect were clearly given by the state authorities concerned, and the record was primarily devoted to this warning. In *Konigsberg*, on the contrary, the Court had ruled that there was inadequate notice of the consequences of refusal to answer questions, and the official action had not been based on mere refusal to answer, but rather on inferences impermissibly drawn from the refusal.

While *Beilan* and *Lerner*, then, did not necessarily undercut *Konigsberg*, they did seem more seriously to challenge the rationale of the *Slochower* decision. But *Slochower* was also distinguished in the 1958 rulings, though perhaps not quite so convincingly. In *Slochower*, so Justice Harlan argued in his *Beilan* opinion, the Fifth

113

Amendment claim had been asserted in a federal inquiry having nothing to do with the qualifications of persons for state employment, whereas in *Beilan* the state had been conducting a direct inquiry into the fitness of its employees.

The uncertainties of this line of cases were not diminished by *Nelson and Globe* v. *County of Los Angeles* (1960), upholding the dismissal of local California employees who had refused to answer a congressional committee's questions about alleged subversive activities. Both employees were social workers in Los Angeles County, one with a permanent and the other with a temporary position. Both invoked the Fifth Amendment in 1956 in refusing to answer questions put by the House Un-American Activities Committee about communist affiliations. A California statute makes it a "duty" of all public employees to answer questions about subversion before state and federal investigatory bodies. Anyone failing to answer "on any ground whatsoever" is deemed "guilty of insubordination" and "shall be suspended and dismissed."

Chief Justice Warren, a Californian, did not participate in either decision. In dealing with Nelson, the permanent employee, the Court voted four to four, thus upholding the state court decision which approved the constitutionality of the dismissal. But in dealing with Globe, the temporary employee, the Court divided five to three in upholding his dismissal. Justice Clark, author of the *Slochower* opinion, was given the job of explaining for the Court the difference between Globe's treatment and Slochower's; the other justices making up the majority were Frankfurter, Harlan, Whittaker, and Stewart.

Clark's theory for accomplishing this difficult feat was that Slochower was discharged under a statute which treated a Fifth Amendment claim as an automatic confession of guilt; this was constitutionally impermissible. Globe, on the other hand, was dismissed for insubordination because he had refused to give information. This was permissible.

Clark's effort thus to exclude the Fifth Amendment from any relationship to the proceeding was rejected by the dissenters — Black, Douglas, and Brennan. As Black said, the insubordination for which

Globe was discharged consisted "exclusively" of his refusal to testify before the congressional committee on grounds of self-incrimination. Brennan dealt with the irrelevance of *Beilan* and *Lerner* to the present ruling. In those cases the justification for dismissal was that the employees' failure to testify prevented the employing bodies from having affirmative evidence on which to base a finding of competence and reliability. But in *Globe* there was no semblance of an administrative procedure to determine the fitness of the employee. There was simply an automatic discharge for refusing to respond just as there had been in *Slochower.*

Perhaps the best comment on the *Nelson and Globe* decision was given in a *New York Times* editorial:

The unlamented Supreme Court ripper bill proposed some years ago by former Senator Jenner included a provision designed, as Senator Jenner frankly stated, to overrule the court's 1956 decision in the case of Harry Slochower, Brooklyn College professor. . . .

What Senator Jenner was unable to achieve the Supreme Court has now virtually accomplished on its own. In a decision on Monday it upheld the dismissal of two Los Angeles County social workers under circumstances about as close to those in the Slochower case as can be imagined. . . . Both were dismissed under a California statute exactly like the New York ordinance in the Slochower case except in one respect: Instead of specifying that employes who refuse to testify at hearings because of possible self-incrimination must be dismissed, the California law requires dismissal of any persons who decline to testify for any reason.

This distinction without a difference was seized upon by the majority to distinguish Monday's decision from the Slochower case. But for all practical purposes the latter must now be regarded as a dead letter. If a state or city is wise enough to avoid putting the term "self-incrimination" explicitly in the law, it is free to punish employes who exercise a privilege granted to them as citizens by the United States Constitution.

The court's retreat is regrettable, first, because it blurs an intelligent and workable rule developed in recent cases — that a public employer is free to question his own employes and pass on their fitness but that he may not act arbitrarily on the basis of something they say, or do not say, to a third party such as an investigating committee. The decision is even more unfortunate because of the cynical way in which the majority of the court paid homage to the Slochower case while robbing it of all meaning. A performance of this kind deprives the Supreme Court of the intellectual respect it needs now more than it ever did, in these demanding times.[3]

What effect these developments have had on the doctrine of the *Konigsberg* case may perhaps not have to be left to conjecture. Following the Supreme Court's decision in 1957, the California supreme court vacated its prior order denying the petition for review and referred the entire matter back to the committee of bar examiners for a rehearing. When Konigsberg was again called before the committee, he was advised that a refusal to answer material questions would obstruct the committee's inquiry and bar his certification. Nevertheless, he persisted in his refusal to answer questions concerning membership in the Communist Party. No incriminating evidence was presented against him. The committee again refused to certify him for admission, and the California supreme court upheld the committee's action, citing the Supreme Court's *Beilan* decision in support. Two judges dissented, charging their colleagues with ignoring the Supreme Court's ruling in the first *Konigsberg* case.

On March 7, 1960, the Supreme Court agreed to review this second refusal to admit Konigsberg to the bar. Until that decision is handed down, it will be uncertain whether anything remains of the "right to silence" asserted in the *Slochower* and original *Konigsberg* decisions. The *Schware* case seems to be the only one in this group which at present imposes definite limitations on states' freedom to deny access to employment.

[3] *The New York Times*, March 2, 1960.

10

⌐⌐⌐⌐⌐⌐⌐⌐⌐⌐⌐⌐⌐⌐⌐⌐⌐⌐⌐⌐⌐⌐⌐⌐⌐⌐⌐⌐

THE FAILURE
TO CURB THE COURT

THE discussion in this volume has not attempted to cover all the areas of controversy in which the Supreme Court was involved by reason of its decisions between 1956 or 1957 and 1960. In concentrating upon the national security cases, it has been necessary to neglect a number of other irritants in legislative-judicial relations during the period. For example, the congressional response to the *Mallory* decision, in which the Court went further in protecting the procedural rights of a convicted rapist than many members of Congress thought proper, was mentioned in the first chapter, but has not been analyzed in detail or placed in the somewhat turbulent setting of prior Supreme Court involvement in local criminal prosecutions. Yet the *Mallory* dispute had an important part in influencing the climate of legislative opinion about the Court in the years under review.

Whereas the Court had been condemned for protecting individual rights in the *Mallory* case, it was pilloried only somewhat less violently, and in part by the same legislators, for *not* protecting individual rights in the case of *Frank* v. *Maryland* (1959). By a five to four vote the Court in this case held that a Baltimore health inspector who had reason to suspect the presence of rats in a private dwelling could demand admission to the house for the purpose of making an inspection without securing a warrant, and the householder was subject to arrest and fine for resisting inspection without a warrant. Adopting the tactic of using any stick to beat a dog, Representative Dale Alford, the segregationist congressman from Little Rock, immediately castigated the decision in the House as a further illustration of the work of the "oath-breaking usurpers" on the Court.[1]

Still another area in which Congress was considerably perturbed by Court decisions related to censorship on grounds of alleged immorality. One decision particularly the subject of controversy was *Kingsley International Pictures* v. *New York* (1959), testing the application of the New York movie censorship statute to the film, "Lady Chatterley's Lover." The Court had invalidated an earlier New York censorship law in the 1952 case of *Burstyn* v. *Wilson*, but apparently on the fairly narrow ground that the standards adopted by the law were too loose and vague. The Court subsequently reversed censorship actions affecting a number of other motion pictures, but without writing any new opinions and consequently without clarifying the rationale for these actions. In the *Kingsley* case, however, the Court finally did supply a reasoned discussion of the censorship issue, though the fact that five concurring opinions were written, all taking exception in greater or lesser degree to Justice Stewart's opinion for the Court, left the issue still less clear than might have been wished.

At least one sentence of the Stewart opinion, however, was clear enough to provoke denunciatory speeches in Congress. Stewart was stating the general case for the First Amendment's protection of the freedom to advocate ideas, and not merely ideas that are conventional or shared by a majority. The First Amendment, he explained, "protects advocacy of the opinion that adultery may sometimes be proper, no less than advocacy of socialism or the single tax." After some blistering comments on this language, Senator Eastland on July 22, 1959, introduced a constitutional amendment which provided: "The right of each State to decide on the basis of its own public policy questions of decency and morality, and to enact legislation with respect thereto, shall not be abridged." [2] Four other

[1] *Congressional Record*, May 5, 1959, p. 6748 (daily ed.).
[2] S. J. Res. 116, 86th Cong.

southern senators — Kefauver, Talmadge, Johnston, and Thurmond — joined in sponsoring this proposed amendment to the Constitution. The ignoring of other controversial Court decisions in order to concentrate upon the Court's national security rulings has been justified because this was the primary field where legislative retaliation was attempted and where the link with the southern attack on the Court for its desegregation decision was most obvious. We are now ready to summarize and explore the meaning of this legislative-judicial experience.

Sources of Supreme Court Strength

By all odds the most dramatic feature of this history is the demonstration it supplied of underlying judicial strength and the sources of support which the Court can rely on in a time of pressure. The startling fact is that a legislative merger of two such potent influence groups as the national security alarmists and the segregationists was unable over a period of four years to pass any of the anti-Court legislation offered, with the sole and limited exception of the Jencks bill. An analysis of this failure suggests that it may be accounted for by the following facts.

Basically, the Court was protected by the respect which is so widely felt for the judicial institution in the United States. This attitude is often rather inchoate and not based on a well formulated understanding of the judicial function. It may grow in part out of unsophisticated assumptions about the "non-political" character of the Supreme Court's role, which are fundamentally in error. But, whether for the right reasons or for the wrong reasons, a great part of opinion in the United States holds that the Supreme Court should be let alone, or rather that it should be subject to influence only in the accepted manner, namely, by use of the appointing power when vacancies occur. This sense of the fitness of things was outraged when Franklin Roosevelt proposed to lay hands on an economically conservative Court in 1937 and, in spite of some changing of sides due to the different direction from which complaints against the Court came, the same feeling protected the Court in 1957. Many who considered the Court to be mistaken in its national security de-

119

cisions nonetheless concluded that it would be an even greater mistake to try to correct these errors by means which would weaken the judicial institution.

In the second place, the attack on the Court failed because of the character and the motives of some of the attackers. To a very considerable degree the legislative opposition to the Court's security decisions was recruited from among southern members of Congress whose main concern was retaliation for the Court's segregation ruling. Unable to muster a majority in Congress on this issue, they sought a more effective expression of their antagonisms by joining in the hue and cry against the security rulings. Their speeches on this subject were often so violent that they must have given pause to more moderate opponents of the Court. Thus Senator Thurmond referred to the Court's rulings as a "Red Bill of Rights." [3] Charges that the members of the Court were participants in a communist conspiracy to take over the country appeared routinely in the pages of the *Congressional Record*, along with personal abuse of the justices. It is paradoxical but probably true that the segregation issue increased the bitterness of the legislative drive against the Court and at the same time guaranteed the defeat of the attack.

A third and related explanation is supplied by the rather obvious exaggerations in the charges made against the Court. It was common practice, as each of the decisions affecting national security issues was handed down, for it to be immediately distorted and misrepresented as a major threat to the national safety. In the case of two of the decisions, this misrepresentation was unfortunately begun by a member of the Court itself, Justice Clark. He pictured the *Jencks* decision as affording to criminals and communists "a Roman holiday for rummaging through confidential information as well as vital national secrets." In *Greene* v. *McElroy* he charged that the Court was in effect holding that private citizens had "a constitutional right to have access to the Government's military secrets."

The Eisenhower administration also shared some of the responsibility for arousing unjustified alarm over certain Supreme Court actions. Particularly in the *Jencks* and the passport cases, adminis-

[3] *Congressional Record*, June 4, 1959, p. 8906 (daily ed.).

trative requests to Congress for legislative action gave lurid and overdrawn accounts of the effect of judicial rulings. These exaggerated danger warnings, from whatever source they came, failed in every case but one to stampede the Congress into an immediate legislative response, and the legislative delays made it possible to get a more balanced view of the problem. Even in the handling of the Jencks bill, which was rushed through Congress on the urgent pleas of the Department of Justice, the Senate insisted on making its own analysis of the situation and substantially modified the language which the Attorney General had proposed.

Finally, it may be suggested that the Court itself contributed to the defeat of the anti-Court legislation by subsequent moderation of the position taken in some of its controversial decisions. The primary example concerns *Watkins* and *Barenblatt*. As already noted, Justice Harlan, the Court's spokesman in *Barenblatt*, went out of his way to mollify congressional sentiment and to place the work of the House Un-American Activities Committee in a much more favorable light than the *Watkins* opinion had done. Again, in *Uphaus* v. *Wyman* Justice Clark managed to draw most of the teeth from both *Nelson* and *Sweezy*. The principle of the *Konigsberg* case was left considerably clouded by the later *Lerner, Beilan,* and *Nelson and Globe* decisions.

Such modifications in the Court's views were no doubt influential in damping the fires of controversy. However, it seems unlikely that this was another "shift in time that saved nine," such as is supposed to have rescued the Court in 1937. The crisis for this Court, as we have seen, came during the last week of the 1958 session of Congress. The danger of retaliatory legislation had largely passed by the time the Court handed down *Barenblatt, Uphaus,* and the other conciliatory decisions. The Court did not "save" itself by these decisions. It had already been saved because a majority in the two houses of Congress was not disposed, for a variety of reasons, to use legislative power to override judicial determinations or to demean the judicial institution.

It seems quite possible that the Supreme Court's victory in this controversy has had the effect of permanently neutralizing what is perhaps the most drastic congressional authority over the Court, the control of its appellate jurisdiction. Senator Jenner may unwittingly have performed a substantial service when he brought in his blunder-buss bill proposing to strip the Court of its appellate jurisdiction in all the national security areas where the Court had handed down decisions adverse to his point of view.

In defense of his bill, Senator Jenner pointed out quite accurately that the right of appeal to the Supreme Court is not a constitutional right and that the Constitution specifically grants to Congress the power to determine the Court's appellate jurisdiction. But he soon discovered that on this matter it is not enough merely to read the words of the Constitution. Senator Butler's amendments to the Jenner bill eliminated the appellate jurisdiction withdrawal in all fields except admission to the bars of the states, but this insistence on the principle of congressional control over the Court's appellate jurisdiction was enough to defeat the Jenner-Butler bill. The American Bar Association, which in 1950 had proposed a constitutional amendment guaranteeing the Supreme Court's appellate jurisdiction in all cases arising under the Constitution, in its 1959 resolutions spoke strongly against congressional use of the withdrawal power under any circumstances.

It may well be argued that the clause in the Constitution giving Congress control over the Court's appellate jurisdiction has in effect now been repealed by the passage of time and by the recognition that exercise of such power would be in the truest sense subversive of the American tradition of an independent judiciary. The language of Article III, section 2, sounded reasonable in 1787, just as did choosing a President by indirect election. Then the Supreme Court was only a few words in an unadopted document. Today it is preeminently the most respected judicial body in the world. For a hundred and fifty years it has been recognized as having the authority to pass on the constitutionality of acts of Congress. It symbolizes the rule of law in a world which has seen too much of executive dictatorship and legislative irresponsibility. Under these conditions Congress can no longer claim with good conscience the authority granted by Article III, section 2, and every time proposals to exercise such authority are rejected, as the Jenner and Butler proposals were rejected by Congress and public opinion, the Court's control over its appellate jurisdiction is correspondingly strengthened.

Thunder on the Right

The first chapter of this study recalled the principal previous occasions when the Supreme Court was under attack. In this concluding appraisal, perhaps the point most deserving of emphasis, and the aspect which most differentiated the recent from the earlier assaults, was the political orientation of the anti-Court forces. In 1857 it was the liberals and abolitionists who condemned the Court as the defender of human slavery. In 1895 it was the radicals of the day, the western "sons of the wild jackass," who pilloried the Court for its deference to accumulated wealth. In 1935 it was the New Dealers who objected because the Court would not concede the power of the federal government under the commerce clause to deal with the causes of a nation-wide depression.

In the recent controversy, however, the Court heard thunder on the right rather than on the left. It was the reputedly conservative sectors of public opinion which sought to curb the Court, and the liberals who defended it. In the liberal view the Court had properly imposed restrictions on legislative security programs which they felt to be grounded in hysteria and acute misconception of the nature of the internal communist threat and the way to fight it. They believed the Court was under attack because, for the first time in its history, it was basing itself on liberal principles and undertaking to defend the freedoms of the First Amendment against illiberal, misconceived, fundamentally unconstitutional legislation or legislative action.

To speak of a conservative attack on the courts sounds like a contradiction in terms. Anyone who thinks of his political or philosophical position as conservative must of necessity find himself in a most anomalous situation when assaulting the judicial institution. For a true conservative should recognize an independent judiciary as one of the most effective and precious conservative forces in our culture. It is an interesting commentary on American conservative thought that some of its principal apostles had no difficulty in supporting and

123

rationalizing the anti-Court campaign. In this connection particular attention must be devoted to the American Bar Association and to the Republican members of Congress.

The role of the Bar Association in the Court fight has already been discussed. Whatever intellectual respectability the drive on the Court possessed was very largely contributed by the Bar Association's resolutions of February, 1959, and the report of the state chief justices. The Bar Association's pronouncements fell far short of the intellectual standards one would expect from such an organization. The resolutions as drafted by the Association's Special Committee on Communist Tactics, Strategy and Objectives constituted, in the words of the *New York Times*, "a collection of vague scare words, of unattributed quotations, of murky inferences drawn from murkier evidence — in short a remarkably un-lawyerlike document." [4]

Perhaps the most glaring evidence of the group's lack of balance and disregard of professional standards was the language of the original resolution which urged Congress to pass remedial legislation "wherever technicalities are invoked against the protection of our Nation." For a group of reputable lawyers thus to denigrate as "technicalities" the protections against the invasion of individual rights embodied in the concept of due process of law — the role and purpose of which lawyers above all others in our society should understand and cherish — indicates how seriously the exhilaration of communist-hunting had deranged their professional judgment.

The resolutions disclaimed any intention "in any way . . . to indicate censure of the Supreme Court." However, the original committee text of the resolutions belied this intention by wording which could only have been chosen to express censure of the Court. One example was the recommendation for remedial legislation "wherever there are reasonable grounds to believe that as a result of court decisions Internal Security [*sic*] is weakened." The House of Delegates found this wording too intemperate, and revised it to read: "wherever there are reasonable grounds to believe that as a result of court decisions weaknesses in Internal Security have been disclosed." Again, the initial text urged Congress to "restore" to the

<hr/>

[4] *The New York Times*, August 31, 1959.

Smith Act meanings opposite to those which the Court had attributed to the statute in the *Yates* decision. The use of the word "restore" implied that the Court had removed from the statute something which Congress had put in it, and the House of Delegates was sufficiently sensitive to the impropriety of such a charge to eliminate this implication by appropriate textual changes.

These various revisions still left the resolutions as a sharp challenge to the Court, and immediately led to charges, such as that by Representative Celler of New York, that the Bar Association had "maligned" the Court. Ross L. Malone, president of the Bar Association, denied these allegations and made the technically correct point that the Congress was being asked to legislate not because the Court's decisions were bad but because they had disclosed deficiencies in the existing legislation. However, this distinction was too subtle to be very effective.

Important voices were raised within the Association itself to counteract the effect of the resolutions. The state bar of California in its 1959 annual convention adopted almost unanimously a resolution expressing "faith and confidence" in the Supreme Court. A special committee of the New York City Bar Association presented a report in June, 1959, charging that the resolutions had caused "confusion and concern," and had left an unfortunate impression that the criticized decisions had "endangered our security" and had revealed the Court as "insufficiently mindful of security needs." The New York committee made its own analysis of the controversial decisions, and found that they had been "based on well established principles of general applicability." The report concluded that "on an over-all consideration of the recent terms of the Court, there is no basis for assuming that the decisions of the Court involving communism are departures from sound principle; represent an unreasonable balance between society's interests in security and in individual rights, or are deleterious to security." [5]

The reactions to the resolutions came to a head at the Bar Association's annual meeting at Miami Beach in August, 1959. The Association's Bill of Rights Committee presented there an analysis

[5] *The New York Times,* June 14, 1959.

125

of the Supreme Court decisions covered in the earlier resolutions, drafted by Professor Arthur Sutherland of the Harvard Law School, which concluded: "On balance, this committee is unable to see any indication that the security of the nation . . . has been impaired by the Supreme Court of the United States." The committee submitted no resolutions, and so no action was called for from the convention. It is the established procedure of the Association that committee reports represent only the views of the committee, but Mr. Loyd Wright of California, a volatile critic of the Court, charged that the report was an effort to undo the resolutions approved by the House of Delegates in February, and moved to table the report. In debate it was pointed out that such a move would be a bad precedent for suppressing views of members, and the motion to table was finally withdrawn.

One can only conjecture as to the effect of this whole experience on the Bar Association. Certainly the attitude of the Committee on Communist Tactics was not changed, but it seems unlikely that the more responsible leaders of the Association can have been happy with the light in which these resolutions placed the organization. Efforts have subsequently been made to counteract the impression resulting from the House of Delegates' endorsement of the committee's one-sided and unbalanced report. President Malone made some strong speeches in support of judicial independence later in 1959, saying that every "thinking citizen" must realize that "it is to the judicial branch of the government that he will turn in the final analysis for the protection of his rights, regardless of who may threaten them." At the Miami convention, the Association significantly awarded its gold medal for service to Grenville Clark, founder of its Bill of Rights Committee and a long-time member of the American Civil Liberties Union.

Conservative thought as represented by Republican congressmen presents an equally disturbing aspect. The Republicans and Democrats in Congress provided a marked contrast in their reaction to the Court issue. Southern Democrats were of course the most vitriolic opponents of the Court, but the non-southern Democratic majority supplied the principal leadership in defense of the Court.

At the crucial point in the struggle, the closing days of the 1958 session, it was the astute management of the Senate majority leader, Lyndon Johnson, which prevented the adoption of anti-Court legislation.

The Republicans, on the other hand, supported the attack on the Court by an overwhelming majority. In a few instances the legislative measures were of course requested by the Eisenhower administration, as in the case of the passport bill. But the Republican attitude was not based on support for their President. The best insight into Republican motivation can be secured in connection with H. R. 3, the preemption bill, which the administration strongly opposed. In the face of a warning by the Republican Attorney General that this bill would seriously endanger long-established business practices and unsettle judicial decisions in many fields, Republican legislators supported it by a large majority. Contrast this reaction with that of a conservative Democrat, Representative Walter, whose anti-communism as manifested by his leadership of the Un-American Activities Committee has been extremely rugged and bitter. Yet, much as he disliked the Court's security decisions, he opposed H. R. 3 because its backers had been unable to explain what it meant, what it would do, or why it was necessary.

On the Court issue the Republican conservatives in Congress displayed, as on many previous issues, an irresponsibility which is impossible to reconcile with a truly conservative approach toward public issues. A McCarthy or a Jenner is of course alien to any conception of conservatism; they can only be accounted for as radicals of the right. Such men are exceptions, but they are symptomatic of an endemic strain of Know-Nothingism, a basic anti-government attitude, in the Republican Party. Given the party divisions of the past half century, it is of course more likely that non-southern radicals of the right will find a home with the Republicans than with the Democrats, but it is still something of a shock to see how wide the appeal of Know-Nothingism runs in the Republican congressional delegation.

Thus on a demonstrably crackpot bill, H. R. 3, drafted by a southern Democrat and opposed by President Eisenhower and Attorney General Rogers, the House Republican Policy Committee nevertheless backed the measure in the 1959 session, and 114 Republicans voted for it, while only 30 followed their own President in opposition to it. On the other side of the aisle, even with the Southerners' solid support for the bill, the Democrats opposed it by a majority of 162 to 111. If the southern congressmen are eliminated, the Democrats were almost unanimously against the bill, which almost four fifths of the Republicans favored. Perhaps the only incident in this long struggle which would dramatize the party division more starkly was the vote on the Jenner-Butler bill in 1958, which saw the Democratic majority leader, a Texan, Lyndon Johnson, voting to uphold the Court while the Republican minority leader, a Californian, Senator Knowland, joined its attackers.

The Court as Policy-Maker

Among the more responsible critics of the Court, perhaps the most common charge during the recent controversy was that it was engaging in judicial legislation or policy-making. The more sophisticated critics of the Court, realizing that it has throughout its history been engaged in policy-making, refined this charge and alleged, as in the report of the state chief justices, that the Court in the national security decisions "tended to adopt the role of policy-maker without proper judicial restraint." What can be said about this complaint?

A review of the decisions discussed in this book makes clear how often the Court's "policy-making" took the form of an interpretation of congressional statutes. This is not unusual; interpretation of statutory language is one of the Court's major responsibilities, and the role calls for the exercise of considerable judicial discretion. The language of statutes is often prolix and unclear. Even when the draftsmanship is excellent, the statute may be worded in generalities which furnish no very definite guide when courts must apply it to the circumstances of particular cases. The decisions which courts must make in giving effect to statutes are of such a discretionary and creative character that judges inevitably become de facto participants in the legislative process.

The Supreme Court was called on to perform tasks of "judicial legislation" in some of the most important and controversial of the national security decisions. In these cases the Court was confronted with conflicting views about the meaning of legislative language or the intention of Congress. In some instances it resolved these conflicts by interpreting the relevant statutes to favor the goals of individual liberty over those of national security. Obviously, this result did not mean that the Court thought national security was unimportant, or that in any contest between freedom and security it would always prefer the former. There were of course many cold war decisions in which the Court did uphold government action. But limiting our attention to decisions which adopted a libertarian interpretation of disputed statutes, what may the Court be fairly described as having done?

In these cases the Court found itself dealing with significant threats to traditional freedoms, in circumstances where it did not itself see such an overwhelming danger to national security as to foreclose further discussion of the government's case for infringing those freedoms. In this situation the Court's "policy" was to interpret the disputed statutes as not authorizing such infringements. By this tactic the Court avoided any immediate decision about the constitutionality of the government's action and the statutes. In effect the Court said to Congress, "Here is an important issue of constitutional freedom. Did you really mean, when you passed these statutes, that they should be used in the way the government is attempting to use them? Even if the government has fairly interpreted your original intention, will you not now take a second look at the matter, illumined as it is with the facts of these particular cases, and say whether that is still your desire and intention?"

By deciding the cases on the ground of statutory interpretation, the Court does delay the achievement of executive and possibly congressional objectives by requiring reconsideration of the issue by Congress, but it leaves the way completely open for Congress to reassert its intentions, if indeed such is the legislative desire. Congress may, upon reconsideration, disagree with the Court's interpretation. It may amend a statute in order to make clear a meaning that the Court had not found in the language. It may adopt a new statute to assert an authority the Court had not discovered in existing legislation. But whether or not the Court's interpretation is accepted by Congress, the judiciary will have made a useful contribution to the legislative process by keeping squarely before Congress some of the major values of the American constitutional system, and will have acted with commendable self-restraint.

The Supreme Court of course retains its full authority, after the problems of statutory meaning are cleared up, and after taking advantage of any other delays which the process of the law allows, to make a forthright challenge of legislative or administrative action on constitutional grounds, thus exercising its highest "policy" power under the Constitution. Several of the Court's national security decisions were based directly on constitutional doctrine, or at least furnished the occasion for the Court to state or apply libertarian constitutional principles. Thus the *Yates* conviction was invalidated in part by the Court's constitutional distinction between advocacy in the realm of ideas, which may not be punished, and advocacy in the sense of a call to forcible action, which may be punished on the basis of a proper showing of danger.

Again, the *Kent* case specifically announced for the first time a new constitutional right, the right to travel. The *Greene* case, though it did not specifically so hold, certainly implied that confrontation and cross-examination were constitutional rights in security hearings. The *Schware* decision established that arbitrary exclusion of persons from the occupation of their choice is contrary to due process. The *Jencks* case reiterated the established principle that a defendant in a criminal prosecution has a certain right of discovery as to materials in the government's possession bearing on the proof of the charges made.

Constitutional pronouncements in a few other national security cases must be given a more guarded statement because of subsequent judicial qualification of their doctrine. This is particularly true of the *Watkins* decision, which was subjected to major reinterpretation by the *Barenblatt* case. The result is that congressional investigating committees can again, as before *Watkins*, assume that their procedures are substantially free from judicial review. With the Court as narrowly divided as it was in *Barenblatt,* prediction is dangerous, but for the present the only residue from *Watkins* would appear to be an increased possibility that congressional committees must concern themselves with demonstrating the pertinency of questions asked to the announced investigative aims of the committee. The *Konigsberg* and *Nelson* decisions have also, though perhaps to a lesser degree, been limited in meaning by later judicial rulings.

As the Court-curbing controversy recedes into the past and the events of recent years are seen in better perspective, there will be fewer who will fail to understand that the Court's "policy" decisions involved no threat to national security. But while the impact on important security functions was slight, the impact of the Court's decisions on national thinking about the relation between individual freedom and national security must be regarded as of great significance. In the national hue and cry against subversives the Supreme Court's was the only powerful voice in the government to insist that congressional goals and administrative programs be measured against constitutional standards. In a variety of ways the Court underlined the wholesome view that national security is not an end justifying every means which is alleged to further that goal. The Court sought to emphasize that the battle against communism internally must proceed within the framework of our traditional democratic principles.

In exercising this restraining influence, in insisting that time be taken for a second look at some of these cold war programs, the Supreme Court was fulfilling the highest function the institution of judicial review is capable of. By the nature of its organization and its traditions, the Court is the unit in our tripartite system which has the best opportunity to resist the heedless pressures of popular hysteria, to insist on a calm consideration of the constitutional case for popular programs.

It is not easy for the Supreme Court, in spite of its organizational independence and its judicial habits, to perform this function. For judges are subject to the same currents of opinion as move legislators, and they largely have the same goals and purposes. Consequently it requires real courage and dedication to the historic role of an independent judiciary for judges to give effect to their doubts or misgivings about legislative programs. It is much easier to resort to one of the many rationalizations always available to justify judicial acquiescence in legislative action. The Court can counsel itself to observe judicial self-restraint. It can reflect that these are essentially political matters, which legislatures are better equipped to decide. It can warn itself against the doctrinaire enforcement of constitutional prohibitions. These are all valid "policy" positions for the judiciary to take, but if endorsed without judgment or courage they can be carried to the point of judicial abdication.

The essay in Court-curbing examined in this volume is an object lesson of the first importance in the risks which judges must be prepared to run if they cannot conscientiously accept the constitutional justifications for a popular governmental program. Such recent decisions as *Barenblatt* and *Uphaus*, in which the Court markedly deferred to the legislature, suggest that the attacks did in fact take some toll of the Court's will to resist. Solicitor General Rankin spoke in March, 1959, concerning the possible indirect effects upon the Court's independence which he feared might result from the anti-Court campaign.

Independence is primary in the administration of justice and we can never be too watchful in protecting it. We would be shocked to learn that the Court had been reached by bribes or other approaches by interested parties either within or outside the government, but long continued, public attacks may cause an even more serious damage to the Court, although it be an insidious and indirect effort to affect its judgment.

The Solicitor General's remarks were addressed particularly to lawyers, and he continued:

The layman cannot fully realize how much the Court means to the preservation of his freedoms and his fundamental rights. But we who labor in the law know that our responsibility for the defense of the Court is therefore incomparably greater. We cannot permit the Court's independence to be undermined by direct or indirect assaults. Nor can we stand by and let the Court suffer for its declaration of some of the finest values in American life; for its recognition that the declared standards must be lived by; for the reaffirmation of the integrity of the individual; and that the state is required to treat its citizens with equality.

One who argues for a strong and independent Supreme Court must be prepared to answer the question, what if the Supreme Court misuses that power? What if the Supreme Court is wrong? This is a real possibility. In fact, the Court has been rather clearly wrong during several periods of American history. But when that happens, the opportunities for correcting the Court are many and effective. They are so effective, in fact, that it is inconceivable that the Court can long maintain a course of decisions which is contrary to the national temper or demands. It is well to recall that it took only two years for the political process to correct the Court when it tried to declare the New Deal unconstitutional. In essence, all that the Court can do with its great power is to enforce a waiting period during which its doctrines are subject to popular consideration. If the judicial reasoning fails to convince the court of public opinion, it will be overridden by Congress or abandoned by the Court itself as new appointees come onto the Court or as the present members bow to the pressures of the times.

That is why discussion of the Supreme Court's role is so important, and why it is so necessary to understand the Court's holdings. Unquestionably it is difficult for the general public, and even for lawyers, to judge the Court on the basis of the principles pronounced in its decisions. It is so much easier to judge it on the basis of the immediate results achieved by a decision. So when a decision keeps a communist from going to jail, it is easy to say that the Court has made a mistake. The correct way to judge that decision, however, is to determine what principle the Court was enforcing which gave this result, and whether that principle is an important one in the achievement and maintenance of constitutional freedoms. When the Court grounds itself on the firm foundation of the Bill of Rights, it is making its maximum contribution to the public welfare and to the national security.

APPENDIXES, SELECTED BIBLIOGRAPHY,
TABLE OF CASES, AND INDEX

APPENDIX 1

RESOLUTIONS OF THE SPECIAL COMMITTEE ON COMMUNIST TACTICS, STRATEGY, AND OBJECTIVES

(Adopted by the House of Delegates, American Bar
Association, February 24, 1959)

Statement of the Board of Governors Transmitting the Report of the Committee to the House:

The Board of Governors herewith transmits to the House of Delegates the report of the Special Committee without any deletions or alterations excepting a minor correction in Recommendation No. 1.

The Board recommends approval by the House of the several recommendations in the report and their transmittal to the Congress of the United States in order to correct legislative defects in the field of internal security revealed by particular decisions cited in the report.

In making its recommendations for approval, the Board does not in any way intend to indicate censure of the Supreme Court nor an attack upon the independence of the judiciary. Indeed, the obligation of the Bar to defend the Supreme Court as an institution is emphasized in the first resolution proposed by the Committee's Report.

The recommendation for approval, in the case of this report as in the case of all other reports of Association Sections and Committees, does not constitute endorsement of statements in the report itself, such statements being those of the individual members of the Committee.

Committee Recommendations

RESOLUTION I

WHEREAS, the Supreme Court of the United States and an independent judiciary created by the Constitution have been and are the ultimate guardians of the Bill of Rights and the protectors of our freedom, and as such it is the duty of the members of the Bar to defend the Institutions of the Judiciary from unfair and unjust attacks; and

WHEREAS, this Association recognizes that sharp differences have been expressed as to the soundness of some of the recent decisions of the United

make and enforce reasonable restrictions on aliens awaiting deportation to prohibit them from engaging in any activities identical or similar to those upon which the aliens' deportation order was based, with the further right fully to interrogate aliens awaiting deportation concerning their subversive associates or activities.

(e) Insure the effectiveness of the Foreign Agents Registration Act of 1948 by a requirement that political propaganda by agents of foreign principals be labeled for what it is where such agents are situated outside the limits of the United States, but nevertheless directly or indirectly disseminate such propaganda within the United States.

RESOLUTION V

WHEREAS, the respective records of the Subcommittee on Internal Security of the Senate Judiciary Committee and of the House Un-American Activities Committee both charged with the duty of investigating internal security and Communist activities are records of accomplishment and great service to the Nation; and

WHEREAS, the continuation of the work of these Committees is essential to the enactment of sound and adequate legislation to safeguard the National and State security;

NOW, THEREFORE, BE IT RESOLVED that the American Bar Association recommends that the House of Representatives continue to maintain a committee to investigate matters relating to National Security with particular emphasis on Communist activities invested with adequate jurisdiction to accomplish its purpose, and that the Senate continue to maintain and support its Subcommittee on Internal Security; and

BE IT FURTHER RESOLVED that such Committees maintain close liaison with the Intelligence and Security Agencies, as well as with the Attorney General of the United States, to the end that they may be kept advised as to legislative needs of the Executive Branch of the Government required to carry out its responsibilities for internal security.

APPENDIX 2

CONFERENCE OF CHIEF JUSTICES
REPORT OF THE COMMITTEE ON FEDERAL-STATE
RELATIONSHIPS AS AFFECTED BY JUDICIAL DECISIONS
(August, 1958)

Background and Perspective

We think it desirable at the outset of this report to set out some points which may help to put the report in proper perspective, familiar or self-evident as these points may be.

First, though decisions of the Supreme Court of the United States have a major impact upon federal-state relationships and have had such an impact since the days of Chief Justice Marshall, they are only a part of the whole structure of these relationships. These relations are, of course, founded upon the Constitution of the United States itself. They are materially affected not only by judicial decisions but in very large measure by Acts of Congress adopted under the powers conferred by the Constitution. They are also affected, or may be affected, by the exercise of the treaty power.

Of great practical importance as affecting federal-state relationships are the rulings and actions of federal administrative bodies. These include the independent agency regulatory bodies, such as the Interstate Commerce Commission, the Federal Power Commission, the Securities and Exchange Commission, the Civil Aeronautics Board, the Federal Communications Commission and the National Labor Relations Board. Many important administrative powers are exercised by the several departments of the Executive Branch, notably the Treasury Department and the Department of the Interior. The scope and importance of the administration of the federal tax laws are, of course, familiar to many individuals and businesses because of their direct impact, and require no elaboration.

Second, when we turn to the specific field of the effect of judicial decisions on federal-state relationships we come at once to the question as to where power should lie to give the ultimate interpretation to the Constitution and to the laws made in pursuance thereof under the authority of the United States. By necessity and by almost universal common consent, these ultimate

141

powers are regarded as being vested in the Supreme Court of the United States. Any other allocation of such power would seem to lead to chaos. (See Judge Learned Hand's most interesting Holmes Lectures on "The Bill of Rights" delivered at the Harvard Law School this year and published by the Harvard University Press.)

Third, there is obviously great interaction between federal legislation and administrative action on the one hand, and decisions of the Supreme Court on the other, because of the power of the Court to interpret and apply Acts of Congress and to determine the validity of administrative action and the permissible scope thereof.

Fourth, whether federalism shall continue to exist, and if so in what form, is primarily a political question rather than a judicial question. On the other hand, it can hardly be denied that judicial decisions, specifically decisions of the Supreme Court, can give tremendous impetus to changes in the allocation of powers and responsibilities as between the federal and the state governments. Likewise, it can hardly be seriously disputed that on many occasions the decisions of the Supreme Court have produced exactly that effect.

Fifth, this Conference has no legal powers whatsoever. If any conclusions or recommendations at which we may arrive are to have any effect, this can only be through the power of persuasion.

Sixth, it is a part of our obligation to seek to uphold respect for law. We do not believe that this goes so far as to impose upon us an obligation of silence when we find ourselves unable to agree with pronouncements of the Supreme Court (even though we are bound by them), or when we see trends in decisions of that Court which we think will lead to unfortunate results. We hope that the expression of our views may have some value. They pertain to matters which directly affect the work of our state courts. In this report we urge the desirability of self-restraint on the part of the Supreme Court in the exercise of the vast powers committed to it. We endeavor not to be guilty ourselves of a lack of due restraint in expressing our concern and, at times, our criticisms in making the comments and observations which follow.

Problems of Federalism

The difference between matters primarily local and matters primarily national was the guiding principle upon which the framers of our national Constitution acted in outlining the division of powers between the national and state governments.

This guiding principle, central to the American federal system, was recognized when the original Constitution was being drawn and was emphasized by de Tocqueville. Under his summary of the federal Constitution he says:

"The first question which awaited the Americans was so to divide the sovereignty that each of the different states which composed the union should continue to govern itself in all that concerned its internal prosperity, while the entire nation, represented by the Union, should continue to form a compact body and to provide for all general exigencies. The problem was a complex and difficult one. It was as impossible to determine beforehand, with any degree of accuracy, the share of authority that each of the two governments was to enjoy as to foresee all the incidents in the life of a nation."

In the period when the Constitution was in the course of adoption the "Federalist" (No. 45) discussed the division of sovereignty between the Union and the States and said: "The powers delegated by the Constitution to the Federal Government are few and defined. Those which are to remain in the State governments are numerous and indefinite. The former will be exercised principally on external objects, as war, peace, negotiation, and foreign commerce. The powers reserved to the several States will extend to all the objects which, in the ordinary course of affairs, concern the internal order and prosperity of the State."

Those thoughts expressed in the "Federalist" of course are those of the general period when both the original Constitution and the Tenth Amendment were proposed and adopted. They long antedated the proposal of the Fourteenth Amendment.

The fundamental need for a system of distribution of powers between national and state governments was impressed sharply upon the framers of our Constitution not only because of their knowledge of the governmental systems of ancient Greece and Rome. They also were familiar with the government of England; they were even more aware of the colonial governments in the original states and the governments of those states after the Revolution. Included in government on this side of the Atlantic was the institution known as the New England town meeting, though it was not in use in all of the states. A town meeting could not be extended successfully to any large unit of population, which, for legislative action, must rely upon representative government.

But it is this spirit of self-government, of *local* self-government, which has been a vital force in shaping our democracy from its very inception.

The views expressed by our late brother, Chief Justice Arthur T. Vanderbilt, on the division of powers between the national and state governments — delivered in his addresses at the University of Nebraska and published under the title "The Doctrine of the Separation of Powers and Its Present Day Significance" — are persuasive. He traced the origins of the doctrine of the separation of powers to four sources: Montesquieu and other political philosophers who preceded him; English constitutional experience; American colonial experience; and the common sense and political wisdom of the Founding Fathers. He concluded his comments on the experiences of the American colonists with the British government with this sentence: "As colonists they had enough of a completely centralized government with no distribution of powers and they were intent on seeing to it that they should never suffer such grievances from a government of their own construction."

His comments on the separation of powers and the system of checks and balances and on the concern of the Founding Fathers with the proper distribution of governmental power between the nation and the several states indicates that he treated them as parts of the plan for preserving the nation on the one side and individual freedom on the other — in other words, that the traditional tripartite vertical division of powers between the legislative, the executive and the judicial branches of government was not an end in itself, but was a means towards an end; and that the horizontal distribution or allocation of powers between national and state governments was also a means towards the same end and was a part of the separation of powers which was accomplished by the federal Constitution. It is a form of the separation of powers with which Montesquieu was not concerned; but the horizontal division of powers, whether thought of as a form of separation of powers or not, was very much in the minds of the framers of the Constitution.

CONGRESS VERSUS THE SUPREME COURT

Two Major Developments in the Federal System

The outstanding development in federal-state relations since the adoption of the national Constitution has been the expansion of the power of the national government and the consequent contraction of the powers of the state governments. To a large extent this is wholly unavoidable and indeed is a necessity, primarily because of improved transportation and communication of all kinds and because of mass production. On the other hand, our Constitution does envision federalism. The very name of our nation indicates that it is to be composed of states. The Supreme Court of a bygone day said in *Texas* v. *White*, 7 Wall. 700, 721 (1868): "The Constitution, in all its provisions, looks to an indestructible Union of indestructible States."

Second only to the increasing dominance of the national government has been the development of the immense power of the Supreme Court in both state and national affairs. It is not merely the final arbiter of the law; it is the maker of policy in many major social and economic fields. It is not subject to the restraints to which a legislative body is subject. There are points at which it is difficult to delineate precisely the line which should circumscribe the judicial function and separate it from that of policy-making. Thus, usually within narrow limits, a court may be called upon in the ordinary course of its duties to make what is actually a policy decision by choosing between two rules, either of which might be deemed applicable to the situation presented in a pending case.

But if and when a court in construing and applying a constitutional provision or a statute becomes a policy maker, it may leave construction behind and exercise functions which are essentially legislative in character, whether they serve in practical effect as a constitutional amendment or as an amendment of a statute. It is here that we feel the greatest concern, and it is here that we think the greatest restraint is called for. There is nothing new in urging judicial self-restraint, though there may be, and we think there is, new need to urge it.

It would be useless to attempt to review all of the decisions of the Supreme Court which have had a profound effect upon the course of our history. It has been said that the Dred Scott decision made the Civil War inevitable. Whether this is really true or not, we need not attempt to determine. Even if it is discounted as a serious overstatement, it remains a dramatic reminder of the great influence which Supreme Court decisions have had and can have. As to the great effect of decisions of that Court on the economic development of the country, see Mr. Justice Douglas' Address on *Stare Decisis*, 49 *Columbia Law Review* 735.

Sources of National Power

Most of the powers of the national government were set forth in the original constitution; some have been added since. In the days of Chief Justice Marshall the supremacy clause of the federal Constitution and a broad construction of the powers granted to the national government were fully developed, and as a part of this development the extent of national control over interstate commerce became very firmly established. The trends established in those days have never ceased to operate and in comparatively recent years have operated at times in a startling manner in the extent to which interstate commerce has been held to be involved, as for example in the familiar case involving an elevator operator in a loft building.

From a practical standpoint the increase in federal revenues resulting from the Sixteenth Amendment (the Income Tax Amendment) has been of great importance. National control over state action in many fields has been vastly expanded by the Fourteenth Amendment.

We shall refer to some subjects and types of cases which bear upon federal-state relationships.

The General Welfare Clause

One provision of the federal Constitution which was included in it from the beginning but which, in practical effect, lay dormant for more than a century, is the general welfare clause. In *United States v. Butler*, 297 U.S. 1, the original Agricultural Adjustment Act was held invalid. An argument was advanced in that case that the general welfare clause would sustain the imposition of the tax and that money derived from the tax could be expended for any purposes which would promote the general welfare. The Court viewed this argument with favor as a general proposition, but found it not supportable on the facts of that case. However, it was not long before that clause was relied upon and applied. See *Steward Machine Co. v. Davis*, 301 U.S. 548, and *Helvering v. Davis*, 301 U.S. 690. In those cases the Social Security Act was upheld and the general welfare clause was relied upon both to support the tax and to support the expenditures of the money raised by the Social Security taxes.

Grants-in-Aid

Closely related to this subject are the so-called grants-in-aid which go back to the Morrill Act of 1862 and the grants thereunder to the so-called land-grant colleges. The extent of grants-in-aid today is very great but questions relating to the wisdom as distinguished from the legal basis for such grants seem to lie wholly in the political field and are hardly appropriate for discussion in this report. Perhaps we should also observe that since the decision of *Massachusetts v. Mellon*, 262 U.S. 447, there seems to be no effective way in which either a state or an individual can challenge the validity of a federal grant-in-aid.

Doctrine of Pre-emption

Many, if not most, of the problems of federalism today arise either in connection with the commerce clause and the vast extent to which its sweep has been carried by the Supreme Court, or they arise under the Fourteenth Amendment. Historically, cases involving the doctrine of pre-emption pertain mostly to the commerce clause. More recently the doctrine has been applied in other fields, notably in the case of *Commonwealth of Pennsylvania v. Nelson*, in which the Smith Act and other federal statutes dealing with Communism and loyalty problems were held to have pre-empted the field and to invalidate or suspend the Pennsylvania anti-subversive statute which sought to impose a penalty for conspiracy to overthrow the government of the United States by force or violence. In that particular case it happens that the decision of the Supreme Court of Pennsylvania was affirmed. That fact, however, emphasizes rather than detracts from the wide sweep now given to the doctrine of pre-emption.

CONGRESS VERSUS THE SUPREME COURT

Labor Relations Cases

In connection with commerce clause cases, the doctrine of pre-emption, coupled with only partial express regulation by Congress, has produced a state of considerable confusion in the field of labor relations.

One of the most serious problems in this field was pointed up or created (depending upon how one looks at the matter) by the Supreme Court's decision in *Amalgamated Association* v. *Wisconsin Employment Relations Board*, 340 U.S. 383, which overturned a state statute aimed at preventing strikes and lockouts in public utilities. This decision left the states powerless to protect their own citizens against emergencies created by the suspension of essential services, even though, as the dissent pointed out, such emergencies were "economically and practically confined to a [single] state."

In two cases decided on May 28, 1958, in which the majority opinions were written by Mr. Justice Frankfurter and Mr. Justice Burton, respectively, the right of an employee to sue a union in a state court was upheld. In *International Association of Machinists* v. *Gonzales*, a union member was held entitled to maintain a suit against his union for damages for wrongful expulsion. In *International Union, United Auto, etc. Workers* v. *Russell*, an employee, who was not a union member, was held entitled to maintain a suit for malicious interference with his employment through picketing during a strike against his employer. Pickets prevented Russell from entering the plant.

Regardless of what may be the ultimate solution of jurisdictional problems in this field, it appears that at the present time there is unfortunately a kind of no-man's land in which serious uncertainty exists. This uncertainty is in part undoubtedly due to the failure of Congress to make its wishes entirely clear. Also, somewhat varying views appear to have been adopted by the Supreme Court from time to time.

In connection with this matter, in the case of *Textile Union* v. *Lincoln Mills*, 353 U.S. 448, the majority opinion contains language which we find somewhat disturbing. That case concerns the interpretation of Section 301 of the Labor Management Relations Act of 1947. Paragraph (a) of that Section provides: "Suits for violation of contracts between an employer and a labor organization representing employees in an industry affecting commerce as defined in this Chapter, or between any such labor organizations, may be brought in any district court of the United States having jurisdiction of the parties, without respect to the amount in controversy or without regard to the citizenship of the parties." Paragraph (b) of the same Section provides in substance that a labor organization may sue or be sued as an entity without the procedural difficulties which formerly attended suits by or against unincorporated associations consisting of large numbers of persons. Section 301 (a) was held to be more than jurisdictional and was held to authorize federal courts to fashion a body of federal law for the enforcement of these collective bargaining agreements and to include within that body of federal law specific performance of promises to arbitrate grievances under collective bargaining agreements.

What a state court is to do if confronted with a case similar to the *Lincoln Mills* case is by no means clear. It is evident that the substantive law to be applied must be federal law, but the question remains, where is that federal law to be found? It will probably take years for the development or the "fashioning" of the body of federal law which the Supreme Court says the federal courts are authorized to make. Can a state court act at all? If it can act and

146

does act, what remedies should it apply? Should it use those afforded by state law, or is it limited to those which would be available under federal law if the suit were in a federal court? It is perfectly possible that these questions will not have to be answered, since the Supreme Court may adopt the view that the field has been completely pre-empted by the federal law and committed solely to the jurisdiction of the federal courts, so that the state courts can have no part whatsoever in enforcing rights recognized by Section 301 of the Labor Management Relations Act. Such a result does not seem to be required by the language of Section 301 nor yet does the legislative history of that Section appear to warrant such a construction.

Professor Meltzer's monograph has brought out many of the difficulties in this whole field of substantive labor law with regard to the division of power between state and federal governments. As he points out much of this confusion is due to the fact that Congress has not made clear what functions the states may perform and what they may not perform. There are situations in which the particular activity involved is prohibited by federal law, others in which it is protected by federal law, and others in which the federal law is silent. At the present time there seems to be one field in which state action is clearly permissible. That is where actual violence is involved in a labor dispute.

State Law in Diversity Cases

Not all of the decisions of the Supreme Court in comparatively recent years have limited or tended to limit the power of the states or the effect of state laws. The celebrated case of *Erie R. R. v. Tompkins*, 304 U.S. 64, overruled *Swift* v. *Tyson* and established substantive state law, decisional as well as statutory, as controlling in diversity cases in the federal courts. This marked the end of the doctrine of a federal common law in such cases.

In Personam Jurisdiction Over Non-Residents

Also, in cases involving the *in personam* jurisdiction of state courts over non-residents, the Supreme Court has tended to relax rather than tighten restrictions under the due process clause upon state action in this field. *International Shoe Co.* v. *Washington*, 326 U.S. 310, is probably the most significant case in this development. In sustaining the jurisdiction of a Washington court to render a judgment *in personam* against a foreign corporation which carries on some activities within the State of Washington, Chief Justice Stone used the now familiar phrase that there "were sufficient contacts or ties with the State of the forum to make it reasonable and just, according to our traditional conception of fair play and substantial justice, to enforce the obligation which appellant has incurred there." Formalistic doctrines or dogmas have been replaced by a more flexible and realistic approach, and this trend has been carried forward in subsequent cases leading up to and including *McGee* v. *International Life Insurance Co.*, 355 U.S. 220, until halted by *Hanson* v. *Denckla*, 357 U.S. decided June 23, 1958.

Taxation

In the field of taxation the doctrine of intergovernmental immunity has been seriously curtailed partly by judicial decisions and partly by statute. This has not been entirely a one-way street.

In recent years cases involving state taxation have arisen in many fields.

147

Sometimes they have involved questions of burdens upon interstate commerce or the export-import clause, sometimes of jurisdiction to tax as a matter of due process, and sometimes they have arisen on the fringes of governmental immunity, as where a state has sought to tax a contractor doing business with the national government. There have been some shifts in holdings. On the whole, the Supreme Court seems perhaps to have taken a more liberal view in recent years towards the validity of state taxation than it formerly took.

Other Fourteenth Amendment Cases

In many other fields, however, the Fourteenth Amendment has been invoked to cut down state action. This has been noticeably true in cases involving not only the Fourteenth Amendment but also the First Amendment guarantee of freedom of speech or the Fifth Amendment protection against self-incrimination. State anti-subversive acts have been practically eliminated by *Pennsylvania* v. *Nelson* in which the decision was rested on the ground of pre-emption of the field by the federal statutes.

The Sweezy Case — State Legislative Investigations

One manifestation of this restrictive action under the Fourteenth Amendment is to be found in *Sweezy* v. *New Hampshire*, 354 U.S. 234. In that case, the State of New Hampshire had enacted a subversive activity statute which imposed various disabilities on subversive persons and subversive organizations. In 1953 the legislature adopted a resolution under which it constituted the Attorney General a one-man legislative committee to investigate violations of that Act and to recommend additional legislation. Sweezy, described as a non-Communist Marxist, was summoned to testify at the investigation conducted by the Attorney General, pursuant to this authorization. He testified freely about many matters but refused to answer two types of questions: (1) inquiries concerning the activities of the Progressive Party in the state during the 1948 campaign, and (2) inquiries concerning a lecture Sweezy had delivered in 1954 to a class at the University of New Hampshire. He was adjudged in contempt by a state court for failure to answer these questions. The Supreme Court reversed the conviction, but there is no majority opinion. The opinion of the Chief Justice, in which he was joined by Justices Black, Douglas and Brennan, started out by reaffirming the position taken in *Watkins* v. *United States*, 354 U.S. 178, that legislative investigations can encroach on First Amendment rights. It then attacked the New Hampshire Subversive Activities Act and stated that the definition of subversive persons and subversive organizations was so vague and limitless that they extended to "conduct which is only remotely related to actual subversion and which is done free of any conscious intent to be a part of such activity." Then followed a lengthy discourse on the importance of academic freedom and political expression. This was not, however, the ground upon which these four Justices ultimately relied for their conclusion that the conviction should be reversed. The Chief Justice said in part: "The respective roles of the legislature and the investigator thus revealed are of considerable significance to the issue before us. It is eminently clear that the basic discretion of determining the direction of the legislative inquiry has been turned over to the investigative agency. The Attorney General has been given such a sweeping and uncertain mandate that it is his discretion which picks out the subjects that will be pursued, what witnesses will be summoned and what questions will be asked. In this circumstance, it can not be stated authoritatively that the legislature asked the Attorney General to gather the kind of facts comprised in the subjects upon which petitioner was interrogated."

Four members of the Court, two in a concurring opinion and two in a dissenting opinion, took vigorous issue with the view that the conviction was invalid because of the legislature's failure to provide adequate standards to guide the Attorney General's investigation. Mr. Justice Frankfurter and Mr. Justice Harlan concurred in the reversal of the conviction on the ground that there was no basis for a belief that Sweezy or the Progressive Party threatened the safety of the state and hence that the liberties of the individual should prevail. Mr. Justice Clark, with whom Mr. Justice Burton joined, arrived at the opposite conclusion and took the view that the state's interest in self-preservation justified the intrusion into Sweezy's personal affairs.

In commenting on this case Professor Cramton says: "The most puzzling aspect of the Sweezy case is the reliance by the Chief Justice on delegation of power conceptions. New Hampshire had determined that it wanted the information which Sweezy refused to give; to say that the State has not demonstrated that it wants the information seems so unreal as to be incredible. The State had delegated power to the Attorney General to determine the scope of inquiry within the general subject of subversive activities. Under these circumstances the conclusion of the Chief Justice that the vagueness of the resolution violates the due process clause must be, despite his protestations, a holding that a state legislature cannot delegate such a power."

Public Employment Cases

There are many cases involving public employment and the question of disqualification therefor by reason of Communist Party membership or other questions of loyalty. *Slochower* v. *Board of Higher Education*, 350 U.S. 551, is a well known example of cases of this type. Two more recent cases, *Lerner* v. *Casey*, and *Beilan* v. *Board of Public Education*, both in 357 U.S. and decided on June 30, 1958, have upheld disqualifications for employment where such issues were involved, but they did so on the basis of lack of competence or fitness. Lerner was a subway conductor in New York and Beilan was a public school instructor. In each case the decision was by a 5 to 4 majority.

Admission to the Bar

When we come to the recent cases on admission to the bar, we are in a field of unusual sensitivity. We are well aware that any adverse comment which we may make on those decisions lays us open to attack on the grounds that we are complaining of the curtailment of our own powers and that we are merely voicing the equivalent of the ancient protest of the defeated litigant — in this instance the wail of a judge who has been reversed. That is a prospect which we accept in preference to maintaining silence on a matter which we think cannot be ignored without omitting an important element of the subject with which this report is concerned.

Konigsberg v. *State Bar of California*, 353 U.S. 252, seems to us to reach the high water mark so far established by the Supreme Court in overthrowing the action of a state and in denying to a state the power to keep order in its own house.

The majority opinion first hurdled the problem as to whether or not the federal question sought to be raised was properly presented to the state highest court for decision and was decided by that court. Mr. Justice Frankfurter dissented on the ground that the record left it doubtful whether this jurisdictional requirement for review by the Supreme Court had been met and favored a remand of the case for certification by the state highest court of "whether or not it did in fact pass on a claim properly before it under the Due Process Clause of the Fourteenth Amendment." Mr. Justice Harlan and Mr. Justice Clark shared Mr. Justice Frankfurter's jurisdictional views. They also dissented on the merits in an opinion written by Mr. Justice Harlan, of which more later.

The majority opinion next turned to the merits of Konigsberg's application for admission to the bar. Applicable state statutes required one seeking admission to show that he was a person of good moral character and that he did not advocate the overthrow of the national or state government by force or violence. The Committee of Bar Examiners, after holding several hearings on Konigsberg's application, notified him that his application was denied because he did not show that he met the above qualifications.

The Supreme Court made its own review of the facts.

On the score of good moral character, the majority found that Konigsberg had sufficiently established it, that certain editorials written by him attacking this country's participation in the Korean War, the actions of political leaders, the influence of "big business" on American life, racial discrimination and the Supreme Court's decision in *Dennis* v. *United States*, 341 U.S. 494, would not support any rational inference of bad moral character, and that his refusal to answer questions "almost all" of which were described by the Court as having "concerned his political affiliations, editorials and beliefs" (353 U.S. 269) would not support such an inference either. On the matter of advocating the overthrow of the national or state government by force or violence, the Court held (as it had in the companion case of *Schware* v. *Board of Bar Examiners of New Mexico*, 353 U.S. 232, decided contemporaneously) that past membership in the Communist Party was not enough to show bad moral character. The majority apparently accepted as sufficient Konigsberg's denial of any present advocacy of the overthrow of the government of the United States or of California, which was uncontradicted on the record. He had refused to answer questions relating to his past political affiliations and beliefs, which the Bar Committee might have used to test the truthfulness of his present claims. His refusal to answer was based upon his views as to the effect of the First and Fourteenth Amendments. The Court did not make any ultimate determination of their correctness, but (at 353 U.S. 270) said that prior decisions by this Court indicated that his objections to answering the questions (which we shall refer to below) were "not frivolous."

The majority asserted that Konigsberg "was not denied admission to the California Bar simply because he refused to answer questions." In a footnote appended to this statement it is said (353 U.S. 259): "Neither the Committee as a whole nor any of its members ever intimated that Konigsberg would be barred just because he refused to answer relevant inquiries or because he was obstructing the Committee. Some members informed him that they did not necessarily accept his position that they were not entitled to inquire into his political associations and opinions and said that his failure to answer would have some bearing on their determination whether he was qualified. But they never suggested that his failure to answer their questions was, by itself, a sufficient independent ground for denial of his application."

Mr. Justice Harlan's dissent took issue with these views — convincingly, we think. He quoted lengthy extracts from the record of Konigsberg's hearings before the subcommittee and the committee of the State Bar investigating his application. (353 U.S. 284–309.) Konigsberg flatly refused to state whether or not at the time of the hearing he was a member of the Communist Party and refused to answer questions on whether he had ever been a Communist or belonged to various organizations, including the Communist Party. The Bar Committee conceded that he could not be required to answer a question if the answer might tend to incriminate him; but Konigsberg did not stand on the Fifth Amendment and his answer which came nearest to raising that question, as far as we can see, seems to have been based upon a fear of prosecution for perjury for whatever answer he might then give as to membership in the Communist Party. We think, on the basis of the extracts from the record contained in Mr. Justice Harlan's dissenting opinion that the Committee was concerned with its duty under the statute "to certify as to this applicant's good moral character" (p. 295), and that the Committee was concerned with the applicant's "disinclination" to respond to questions proposed by the Committee (p. 301), and that the Committee, in passing on his good moral character, sought to test his veracity (p. 303).

The majority, however, having reached the conclusion above stated, that Konigsberg had not been denied admission to the bar simply because he refused to answer questions, then proceeded to demolish a straw man by saying that there was nothing in the California statutes or decisions, or in the rules of the Bar Committee which had been called to the Court's attention, suggesting that a failure to answer questions "is *ipso facto*, a basis for excluding an applicant from the Bar, irrespective of how overwhelming is his showing of good character or loyalty or how flimsy are the suspicions of the Bar Examiners." Whether Konigsberg's "overwhelming" showing of his own good character would have been shaken if he had answered the relevant questions which he refused to answer, we cannot say. We have long been under the impression that candor is required of members of the bar and, prior to *Konigsberg* we should not have thought that there was any doubt that a candidate for admission to the bar should answer questions as to matters relating to his fitness for admission, and that his failure or refusal to answer such questions would warrant an inference unfavorable to the applicant or a finding that he had failed to meet the burden of proof of his moral fitness.

Let us repeat that Konigsberg did not invoke protection against self-incrimination. He invoked a privilege which he claimed to exist against answering certain questions. These might have served to test his veracity at the Committee hearings held to determine whether or not he was possessed of the good moral character required for admission to the bar.

The majority opinion seems to ignore the issue of veracity sought to be raised by the questions which Konigsberg refused to answer. It is also somewhat confusing with regard to the burden of proof. At one point (pp. 270–271) it says that the Committee was not warranted in drawing from Konigsberg's refusal to answer questions any inference that he was of bad moral character; at another (p. 273) it says that there was no evidence in the record to justify a finding that he had failed to establish his good moral character.

Also at page 273 of 353 U.S., the majority said: "We recognize the importance of leaving States free to select their own bars, but it is equally important that the State not exercise this power in an arbitrary or discriminatory manner nor in such way as to impinge on the freedom of political expression or association. A bar composed of lawyers of good character is a worthy objective but it is unnecessary to sacrifice vital freedoms in order to obtain that goal. It is also important to society and the bar itself that lawyers be unintimidated — free to think, speak and act as members of an Independent Bar." The majority thus makes two stated concessions — each, of course, subject to limitations — one, that it is important to leave the states free to select their own bars and the other, that "a bar composed of lawyers of good character is a worthy objective."

We think that Mr. Justice Harlan's dissent on the merits, in which Mr. Justice Clark joined, shows the fallacies of the majority position. On the facts which we think were demonstrated by the excerpts from the record included in that dissent, it seems to us that the net result of the case is that a state is unable to protect itself against admitting to its bar an applicant who, by his own refusal to answer certain questions as to what the majority regarded as "political" associations and activities, avoids a test of his veracity through cross-examination on a matter which he has the burden of proving in order to establish his right to admission to the bar. The power left to the states to regulate admission to their bars under *Konigsberg* hardly seems adequate to achieve what the majority chose to describe as a "worthy objective" — "a bar composed of lawyers of good character."

We shall close our discussion of *Konigsberg* by quoting two passages from Mr. Justice Harlan's dissent, in which Mr. Justice Clark joined. In one, he states that "this case involves an area of federal-state relations — the right of States to establish and administer standards for admission to their bars — into which this Court should be especially reluctant and slow to enter." In the other, his concluding comment (p. 312), he says: "[W]hat the Court has really done, I think, is simply to impose on California its own notions of public policy and judgment. For me, today's decision represents an unacceptable intrusion into a matter of State concern."

The *Lerner* and *Beilan* cases above referred to seem to indicate some recession from the intimations, though not from the decisions, in the *Konigsberg* and *Slochower* cases. In *Beilan* the school teacher was told that his refusal to answer questions might result in his dismissal, and his refusal to answer questions pertaining to loyalty matters was held relevant to support a finding that he was incompetent. "Incompetent" seems to have been taken in the sense of unfit.

State Administration of Criminal Law

When we turn to the impact of decisions of the Supreme Court upon the state administration of criminal justice, we find that we have entered a very broad field. In many matters, such as the fair drawing of juries, the exclusion of forced confessions as evidence, and the right to counsel at least in all serious cases, we do not believe that there is any real difference in doctrine between the views held by the Supreme Court of the United States and the views held by the highest courts of the several States. There is, however, a rather considerable difference at times as to how these general principles should be applied and as to whether they have been duly regarded or not. In such matters the Supreme Court not only feels free to review the facts, but considers it to be its duty to make an independent review of the facts. It sometimes seems that the rule which governs most appellate courts in the view of findings of fact by trial courts is given lip service, but is actually given the least possible practical effect. Appellate courts generally will give great weight to the findings of fact by trial courts which had the opportunity to see and hear the witnesses, and they are reluctant to disturb such findings. The Supreme Court at times seems to read the records in criminal cases with a somewhat different point of view. Perhaps no more striking example of this can readily be found than in *Moore* v. *Michigan*, 355 U.S.155.

In the *Moore* case the defendant had been charged in 1937 with the crime of first degree murder, to which he pleaded guilty. The murder followed a rape and was marked by extreme brutality. The defendant was a Negro youth, 17 years of age at the time of the offense, and is described as being of limited education (only the 7th grade) and as being of rather low mentality. He confessed the crime to law enforcement officers and he expressed a desire to plead guilty and "get it over with." Before such a plea was permitted to be entered he was interviewed by the trial judge in the privacy of the judge's chambers and he again admitted his guilt, said he did not want counsel and expressed the desire to "get it over with," to be sent to whatever institution he was to be confined in, and to be placed under observation. Following this, the plea of guilty was accepted and there was a hearing to determine the punishment which should be imposed. About 12 years later the defendant sought a new trial principally on the ground that he had been unfairly dealt with because he was not represented by counsel. He had expressly disclaimed any desire for counsel at the time of his trial. Pursuant to the law of Michigan, he had a hearing on this application for a new trial. In most respects his testimony was seriously at variance with the testimony of other witnesses. He was corroborated in one matter by a man who had been a deputy sheriff at the time when the prisoner was arrested and was being questioned. The trial court, however, found in substance that the defendant knew what he was doing when he rejected the appointment of counsel and pleaded guilty, that he was then calm and not intimidated, and, after hearing him testify, that he was completely unworthy of belief. It accordingly denied the application for a new trial. This denial was affirmed by the Supreme Court of Michigan, largely upon the basis of the findings of fact by the trial court. The Supreme Court of the United States reversed. The latter Court felt that counsel might have been of assistance to the prisoner, in view of his youth, lack of education and low mentality, by requiring the state to prove its case against him (saying the evidence was largely circumstantial), by raising a question as to his sanity, and by presenting factors which might have lessened the severity of the penalty imposed. It was the maximum permitted under the Michigan law — solitary confinement for life at hard labor. The case was decided by the Supreme Court of the United States in 1957. The majority opinion does not seem to have given any consideration whatsoever to the difficulties of proof which the state might encounter after the lapse of many years or the risks to society which might result from the release of a prisoner of this type, if the new prosecution should fail. They are, however, pointed out in the dissent.

Another recent case which seems to us surprising, and the full scope of which we cannot foresee, is *Lambert* v. *California*, 355 U.S., decided December 16, 1957. In that case a majority of the Court reversed a conviction under a Los Angeles ordinance which required a person convicted of a felony, or

153

of a crime which would be felony under the law of California, to register upon taking up residence in Los Angeles. Lambert had been convicted of forgery and had served a long term in a California prison for that offense. She was arrested on suspicion of another crime and her failure to register was then discovered and she was prosecuted, convicted and fined. The majority of the Supreme Court found that she had no notice of the ordinance, that it was not likely to be known, that it was a measure merely for the convenience of the police, that the defendant had no opportunity to comply with it after learning of it and before being prosecuted, that she did not act wilfully in failing to register, that she was not "blameworthy" in failing to do so, and that her conviction involved a denial of due process of law.

This decision was reached only after argument and reargument. Mr. Justice Frankfurter wrote a short dissenting opinion in which Mr. Justice Harlan and Mr. Justice Whittaker joined. He referred to the great number of state and federal statutes which imposed criminal penalties for non-feasance and stated that he felt confident that "the present decision will turn out to be an isolated deviation from the strong current of precedents — a derelict on the waters of the law."

We shall not comment in this report upon the broad sweep which the Supreme Court now gives to habeas corpus proceedings. Matters of this sort seem to fall within the scope of the Committee of this Conference on the Habeas Corpus Bill which has been advocated for some years by this Conference for enactment by the Congress of the United States, and has been supported by the Judicial Conference of the United States, the American Bar Association, the Association of Attorneys General and the Department of Justice.

We cannot, however, completely avoid any reference at all to habeas corpus matters because what is probably the most far reaching decision of recent years on state criminal procedure which has been rendered by the Supreme Court is itself very close to a habeas corpus case. That is the case of *Griffin* v. *Illinois*, 351 U.S. 12, which arose under the Illinois Post Conviction Procedure Act. The substance of the holding in that case may perhaps be briefly and accurately stated in this way: If a transcript of the record, or its equivalent, is essential to an effective appeal, and if a state permits an appeal by those able to pay for the cost of the record or its equivalent, then the state must furnish without expense to an indigent defendant either a transcript of the record at his trial, or an equivalent thereof, in order that the indigent defendant may have an equally effective right of appeal. Otherwise, the inference seems clear, the indigent defendant must be released upon habeas corpus or similar proceedings. Probably no one would dispute the proposition that the poor man should not be deprived of the opportunity for a meritorious appeal simply because of his poverty. The practical problems which flow from the decision in *Griffin* v. *Illinois* are, however, almost unlimited and are now only in course of development and possible solution. This was extensively discussed at the 1957 meeting of this Conference of Chief Justices in New York.

We may say at this point that in order to give full effect to the doctrine of *Griffin* v. *Illinois*, we see no basis for distinction between the cost of the record and other expenses to which the defendant will necessarily be put in the prosecution of an appeal. These include filing fees, the cost of printing the brief and of such part of the record as may be necessary, and counsel fees.

154

The *Griffin* case was very recently given retroactive effect by the Supreme Court in a per curiam opinion in *Eskridge* v. *Washington State Board of Prison Terms and Paroles,* 78 S. Ct. 1061. In that case the defendant, who was convicted in 1935, gave timely notice of an appeal. His application then made for a copy of the transcript of the trial proceedings to be furnished at public expense was denied by the trial judge. A statute provided for so furnishing a transcript if "in his [the trial judge's] opinion justice will thereby be promoted." The trial judge found that justice would not be promoted, in that the defendant had had a fair and impartial trial, and that, in his opinion, no grave or prejudicial errors had occurred in the trial. The defendant then sought a writ of mandate from the Supreme Court of the state, ordering the trial judge to have the transcript furnished for the prosecution of his appeal. This was denied and his appeal was dismissed. In 1956 he instituted habeas corpus proceedings which, on June 16, 1958, resulted in a reversal of the Washington Court's decision and a remand "for further proceedings not inconsistent with this opinion." It was conceded that the "reporter's transcript" from the trial was still available. In what form it exists does not appear from the Supreme Court's opinion. As in *Griffin,* it was held that an adequate substitute for the transcript might be furnished in lieu of the transcript itself. Justices Harlan and Whittaker dissented briefly on the ground that "on this record the Griffin case decided in 1956 should not be applied to this conviction occurring in 1935." This accords with the view expressed by Mr. Justice Frankfurter in his concurring opinion in *Griffin* that it should not be retroactive. He did not participate in the *Eskridge* case.

Just where *Griffin* v. *Illinois* may lead us is rather hard to say. That it will mean a vast increase in criminal appeals and a huge case load for appellate courts seems almost to go without saying. There are two possible ways in which the meritorious appeals might be taken care of and the non-meritorious appeals eliminated. One would be to apply a screening process to appeals of all kinds, whether taken by the indigent or by persons well able to pay for the cost of appeals. It seems very doubtful that legislatures generally would be willing to curtail the absolute right of appeal in criminal cases which now exists in many jurisdictions. Another possible approach would be to require some showing of merit before permitting an appeal to be taken by an indigent defendant at the expense of the state.

Whether this latter approach which we may call "screening" would be practical or not is, to say the least, very dubious. First, let us look at a federal statute and Supreme Court decisions thereunder. What is now subsection (a) of Section 1915 of Title 28, U.S.C.A. contains a sentence reading as follows: "An appeal may not be taken in forma pauperis if the trial court certifies in writing that it is not taken in good faith." This section or a precursor thereof was involved in *Miller* v. *United States,* 317 U.S. 192, *Johnson* v. *United States,* 352 U.S. 565, and *Farley* v. *United States,* 354 U.S. 521, 523. In the *Miller* case the Supreme Court held that the discretion of the trial court in withholding such a certificate was subject to review on appeal, and that in order that such a review might be made by the Court of Appeals it was necessary that it have before it either the transcript of the record or an adequate substitute therefor, which might consist of the trial judge's notes or of an agreed statement as to the points on which review was sought. Similar holdings were made by per curiam opinions in the *Johnson* and *Farley* cases, in each of which the trial court refused to certify that the appeal was taken in good faith. In each case, though perhaps more clearly in *Johnson*, the trial court seems to have felt that the proposed appeal was frivolous, and hence not in good faith.

The *Eskridge* case, above cited, decided on June 16, 1958, rejected the screening process under the state statute there involved, and appears to require, under the Fourteenth Amendment, that a full appeal be allowed — not simply a review of the screening process, as under the federal statute above cited. The effect of the *Eskridge* case thus seems rather clearly to be that unless all appeals, at least in the same types of cases, are subject to screening, none may be.

It would seem that it may be possible to make a valid classification of appeals which shall be subject to screening and of appeals which shall not. Such a classification might be based upon the gravity of the offense or possibly upon the sentence imposed. In most, if not all, states, such a classification would doubtless require legislative action.

In the *Griffin* case, it will be recalled, the Supreme Court stated that a substitute for an actual transcript of the record would be acceptable if it were sufficient to present the points upon which the defendant based his appeal. The Supreme Court suggested the possible use of bystanders' bills of exceptions.

It seems probable to us that an actual transcript of the record will be required in most cases. For example, in cases where the basis for appeal is the alleged insufficiency of the evidence, it may be very difficult to eliminate from that part of the record which is to be transcribed portions which seem to have no immediate bearing upon this question. A statement of the facts to be agreed upon by trial counsel for both sides may be still more difficult to achieve even with the aid of the trial judge.

The danger of swamping some state appellate courts under the flood of appeals which may be loosed by *Griffin* and *Eskridge* is not a reassuring prospect. How far *Eskridge* may lead and whether it will be extended beyond its facts remain to be seen.

Conclusions

This long review, though far from exhaustive, shows some of the uncertainties as to the distribution of power which are probably inevitable in a federal system of government. It also shows, on the whole, a continuing and, we think, an accelerating trend towards increasing power of the national government and correspondingly contracted power of the state governments. Much of this is doubtless due to the fact that many matters which were once mainly of local concern are now parts of larger matters which are of national concern. Much of this stems from the doctrine of a strong, central government and of the plenitude of national power within broad limits of what may be "necessary and proper" in the exercise of the granted powers of the national government which was expounded and established by Chief Justice Marshall and his colleagues, though some of the modern extensions may and do seem to us to go to extremes. Much, however, comes from the extent of the control over the action of the states which the Supreme Court exercises under its views of the Fourteenth Amendment.

We believe that strong state and local governments are essential to the effective functioning of the American system of federal government; that they should not be sacrificed needlessly to leveling, and sometimes deadening, uniformity; and that in the interest of active, citizen participation in self-government — the foundation of our democracy — they should be sustained and strengthened.

As long as this country continues to be a developing country and as long as the conditions under which we live continue to change, there will always be problems of the allocation of power depending upon whether certain matters should be regarded as primarily of national concern or as primarily of local concern. These adjustments can hardly be effected without some friction. How much friction will develop depends in part upon the wisdom of those empowered to alter the boundaries and in part upon the speed with which such changes are effected. Of course, the question of speed really involves the exercise of judgment and the use of wisdom, so that the two things are really the same in substance.

We are now concerned specifically with the effect of judicial decisions upon the relations between the federal government and the state governments. Here we think that the overall tendency of decisions of the Supreme Court over the last 25 years or more has been to press the extension of federal power and to press it rapidly. There have been, of course, and still are, very considerable differences within the Court on these matters, and there has been quite recently a growing recognition of the fact that our government is still a federal government and that the historic line which experience seems to justify between matters primarily of national concern and matters primarily of local concern should not be hastily or lightly obliterated. A number of justices have repeatedly demonstrated their awareness of problems of federalism and their recognition that federalism is still a living part of our system of government.

The extent to which the Supreme Court assumes the function of policy-maker is also of concern to us in the conduct of our judicial business. We realize that in the course of American history the Supreme Court has frequently — one might, indeed, say customarily — exercised policy-making powers going far beyond those involved, say, in making a selection between competing rules of law.

We believe that in the fields with which we are concerned, and as to which we feel entitled to speak, the Supreme Court too often has tended to adopt the role of policy-maker without proper judicial restraint. We feel this is particularly the case in both of the great fields we have discussed — namely, the extent and extension of the federal power, and the supervision of state action by the Supreme Court by virtue of the Fourteenth Amendment. In the light of the immense power of the Supreme Court and its practical non-reviewability in most instances no more important obligation rests upon it, in our view, than that of careful moderation in the exercise of its policy-making role.

We are not alone in our view that the Court, in many cases arising under the Fourteenth Amendment, has assumed what seem to us primarily legislative powers. (See Judge Learned Hand on the Bill of Rights.) We do not believe that either the framers of the original Constitution or the possibly somewhat less gifted draftsmen of the Fourteenth Amendment ever contemplated that the Supreme Court would, or should, have the almost unlimited policy-making powers which it now exercises. It is strange, indeed, to reflect that under a constitution which provides for a system of checks and balances and of distribution of power between national and state governments one branch of one government — the Supreme Court — should attain the immense, and in many respects, dominant, power which it now wields.

157

We believe that the great principle of distribution of powers among the various branches of government and between levels of government has vitality today and is the crucial base of our democracy. We further believe that in construing and applying the Constitution and laws made in pursuance thereof, this principle of the division of power based upon whether a matter is primarily of national or of local concern should not be lost sight of or ignored, especially in fields which bear upon the meaning of a constitutional or statutory provision, or the validity of state action presented for review. For, with due allowance for the changed conditions under which it may or must operate, the principle is as worthy of our consideration today as it was of the consideration of the great men who met in 1787 to establish our nation as a nation.

It has long been an American boast that we have a government of laws and not of men. We believe that any study of recent decisions of the Supreme Court will raise at least considerable doubt as to the validity of that boast. We find first that in constitutional cases unanimous decisions are comparative rarities and that multiple opinions, concurring or dissenting, are common occurrences. We find next that divisions in result on a 5 to 4 basis are quite frequent. We find further that on some occasions a majority of the Court cannot be mustered in support of any one opinion and that the result of a given case may come from the divergent views of individual Justices who happen to unite on one outcome or the other of the case before the Court.

We further find that the Court does not accord finality to its own determinations of constitutional questions, or for that matter of others. We concede that a slavish adherence to *stare decisis* could at times have unfortunate consequences; but it seems strange that under a constitutional doctrine which requires all others to recognize the Supreme Court's rulings on constitutional questions as binding adjudications of the meaning and application of the Constitution, the Court itself has so frequently overturned its own decisions thereon, after the lapse of periods varying from one year to seventy-five, or even ninety-five years. (See the tables appended to Mr. Justice Douglas' address on *Stare Decisis*, 49 *Columbia Law Review* 735, 756–758.) The Constitution expressly sets up its own procedures for amendment, slow or cumbersome though they may be.

These frequent differences and occasional overrulings of prior decisions in constitutional cases cause us grave concern as to whether individual views of the members of the court as from time to time constituted, or of a majority thereof, as to what is wise or desirable do not unconsciously override a more dispassionate consideration of what is or is not constitutionally warranted. We believe that the latter is the correct approach, and we have no doubt that every member of the Supreme Court intends to adhere to that approach, and believes that he does so. It is our earnest hope which we respectfully express, that that great Court exercise to the full its power of judicial self-restraint by adhering firmly to its tremendous, strictly judicial powers and by eschewing, so far as possible, the exercise of essentially legislative powers when it is called upon to decide questions involving the validity of state action, whether it deems such action wise or unwise. The value of our system of federalism, and of local self-government in local matters which it embodies, should be kept firmly in mind, as we believe it was by those who framed our Constitution.

At times the Supreme Court manifests, or seems to manifest, an impatience with the slow workings of our federal system. That impatience may extend to an unwillingness to wait for Congress to make clear its intention to exercise the powers conferred upon it under the Constitution, or the extent to which it undertakes to exercise them, and it may extend to the slow processes of amending the Constitution which that instrument provides. The words of Elihu Root on the opposite side of the problem, asserted at a time when demands were current for recall of judges and Judicial decisions, bear repeating: "If the people of our country yield to impatience which would destroy the system that alone makes effective these great impersonal rules and preserves our constitutional government, rather than endure the temporary inconvenience of pursuing regulated methods of changing the law, we shall not be reforming. We shall not be making progress, but shall be exhibiting that lack of self-control which enables great bodies of men to abide the slow process of orderly government rather than to break down the barriers of order when they are struck by the impulse of the moment." (Quoted in 31 *Boston University Law Review* 43.)

We believe that what Mr. Root said is sound doctrine to be followed towards the Constitution, the Supreme Court and its interpretation of the Constitution. Surely, it is no less incumbent upon the Supreme Court, on its part, to be equally restrained and to be as sure as is humanly possible that it is adhering to the fundamentals of the Constitution with regard to the distribution of powers and the separation of powers, and with regard to the limitations of judicial power which are implicit in such separation and distribution, and that it is not merely giving effect to what it may deem desirable.

We may expect the question as to what can be accomplished by the report of this committee or by resolutions adopted in conformity with it. Most certainly some will say that nothing expressed here would deter a member or group of members of an independent judiciary from pursuing a planned course. Let us grant that this may be true. The value of a firm statement by us lies in the fact that we speak as members of all the state appellate courts with a background of many years' experience in the determination of thousands of cases of all kinds. Surely there are those who will respect a declaration of what we believe. And it just could be true that our statement might serve as an encouragement to those members of an independent judiciary who now or in the future may in their conscience adhere to views more consistent with our own.

Respectfully submitted:

FREDERICK W. BRUNE, Chief Judge of Maryland, Chairman
ALBERT CONWAY, Chief Judge of New York
JOHN R. DETHMERS, Chief Justice of Michigan
WILLIAM H. DUCKWORTH, Chief Justice of Georgia
JOHN E. HICKMAN, Chief Justice of Texas
JOHN E. MARTIN, Chief Justice of Wisconsin
MARTIN A. NELSON, Associate Justice of Minnesota
WILLIAM C. PERRY, Chief Justice of Oregon
TAYLOR H. STUKES, Chief Justice of South Carolina
RAYMOND S. WILKINS, Chief Justice of Massachusetts

SELECTED
BIBLIOGRAPHY

American Bar Association, *Resolutions and Report of the Special Committee on Communist Tactics, Strategy and Objectives.* February, 1959.

Bickel, Alexander, "An Inexplicable Document," *New Republic*, September 29, 1958, pp. 9–11.

———, "Court Curbing Time," *New Republic*, May 25, 1959, pp. 10–12.

Black, Charles L., Jr., *The People and the Court: Judicial Review in a Democracy.* New York: Macmillan, 1960.

Byrnes, James F., "The Supreme Court Must Be Curbed," *U. S. News and World Report*, May 18, 1956, pp. 50ff.

Celler, Emanuel, "The Supreme Court Survives a Barrage," *The Reporter*, November 27, 1958, pp. 31–33.

Chase, Harold W., "The Warren Court and Congress," 44 *Minnesota Law Review* 595–637 (March, 1960).

Conference of Chief Justices, Committee on Federal-State Relationships as Affected by Judicial Decisions, *Report*, August 23, 1958. Reprinted by The Virginia Commission on Constitutional Government, Richmond, Virginia; also by *Harvard Law Record*, October 23, 1958.

"Congress Acts on Supreme Court Decisions," 38 *Congressional Digest* 225–256 (October, 1959).

"Congressional Reversal of Supreme Court Decisions: 1945–1957," 71 *Harvard Law Review* 1324–1337 (May, 1958).

"Controversy Over the Supreme Court," 10 *Syracuse Law Review* 242–270 (Spring, 1959). A symposium.

Dahl, Robert A., "Decision Making in a Democracy: The Role of the Supreme Court as a National Policy Maker," 6 *Journal of Public Law* 279–295 (Fall, 1957).

Elliott, Sheldon D., "Court-Curbing Proposals in Congress," 33 *Notre Dame Lawyer* 597–612 (August, 1958).

Frank, John P., "The Historic Role of the Supreme Court," 48 *Kentucky Law Journal* 26–47 (Fall, 1959).

160

SELECTED BIBLIOGRAPHY

Freund, Paul A., "Storm Over the American Supreme Court," 21 *Modern Law Review* 345–358 (July, 1958).

Gordon, Rosalie M., *Nine Men Against America: The Supreme Court and Its Attack on American Liberties*. New Rochelle: America's Future, Inc., 1957.

Hand, Learned, *The Bill of Rights*. Cambridge: Harvard University Press, 1958.

Horsky, Charles A., "Law Day: Some Reflections on Current Proposals to Curtail the Supreme Court," 42 *Minnesota Law Review* 1105–1111 (May, 1958).

Jaffe, Louis L., "The Court Debated, Another View," *New York Times Magazine*, June 5, 1960, pp. 36ff.

Kalven, Harry Jr., "Mr. Alexander Meiklejohn and the Barenblatt Opinion," 27 *University of Chicago Law Review* 316–340 (Winter, 1960).

Lewis, Anthony, "A Newspaperman's View: The Role of the Supreme Court," 45 *American Bar Association Journal* 911–914ff. (September, 1959).

Losos, J. O., "The Supreme Court and Its Critics: Is the Supreme Court Moving Left?" 21 *Review of Politics* 495–510 (July, 1959).

Mason, Alpheus T., "The Supreme Court: Temple and Forum," 48 *Yale Review* 524–540 (June, 1959).

Meiklejohn, Alexander, "The Barenblatt Opinion," 27 *University of Chicago Law Review* 329–340 (Winter, 1960).

Mendelson, Wallace, "The Court Must Not Be Curbed: A Reply to Mr. Byrnes," 19 *Journal of Politics* 81–86 (February, 1957).

Menez, Joseph F., "A Brief in Support of the Supreme Court," 54 *Northwestern University Law Review* 30–59 (March–April, 1959).

"Moves to Curb the U. S. Supreme Court," 37 *Congressional Digest* 131–160 (May, 1958).

Osborne, John, "One Supreme Court," *Life*, June 16, 1958, pp. 92–94ff.

"Policy Making in a Democracy: The Role of the United States Supreme Court," 6 *Journal of Public Law* 275–508 (Fall, 1957). A symposium.

Pritchett, C. Herman, *The Political Offender and the Warren Court*. Boston: Boston University Press, 1958; also 38 *Boston University Law Review* 53–123 (Winter, 1958).

————, "The Supreme Court Today: Constitutional Interpretation and Judicial Self Restraint," 3 *South Dakota Law Review* 51–79 (Spring, 1958).

"Pro and Con in Growing Debate Over Powers of Supreme Court," *U. S. News and World Report*, October 24, 1958, pp. 110–118.

Rauh, Joseph L., Jr., "The Truth About Congress and the Court," *The Progressive*, November, 1958, pp. 30ff.

Reisman, David, "New Critics of the Court," *New Republic*, July 29, 1957, pp. 9–13.

Rodell, Fred, "Conflict Over the Court," *The Progressive*, December, 1958, pp. 11–13.

————, "The Crux of the Court Hullabaloo," *New York Times Magazine*, May 29, 1960, pp. 13ff.

"The Role of the Supreme Court in the American Constitutional System," 33 *Notre Dame Lawyer* 521–616 (August, 1958). A symposium.

Schwartz, Bernard, "Is Criticism of the High Court Valid?" *New York Times Magazine*, August 25, 1957, pp. 14ff.

Spense, P., "Get the Supreme Court Out of Politics," *American Mercury*, October, 1957, pp. 23–28.

Steamer, Robert J., "Statesmanship or Craftsmanship: Current Conflict Over the Supreme Court," 11 *Western Political Quarterly* 265–277 (June, 1958).

Swisher, Carl B., "Dred Scott One Hundred Years After," 19 *Journal of Politics* 167–183 (1957).

"The Supreme Court," *Time*, July 1, 1957, pp. 11–15.

U. S. Senate, Committee on the Judiciary, *Limitation of the Supreme Court Jurisdiction and Strengthening of Anti-Subversive Laws: Report*, May 15, 1958. Washington: Government Printing Office, 1958.

U. S. Senate, Committee on the Judiciary, Subcommittee to Investigate the Administration of the Internal Security Act and Other Internal Security Laws. *Limitation of the Appellate Jurisdiction of the United States Supreme Court: Hearings on S. 2646*, August 7, 1957–March 5, 1958. Two parts plus appendixes. Washington: Government Printing Office, 1957, 1958.

University of Chicago Law School, "Special Supplement," 8 *The Law School Record* 1–149 (Autumn, 1958). Text of monographs submitted to the Conference of Chief Justices, Committee on Federal-State Relationships as Affected by Judicial Decisions.

Vetter, George M., Jr., "Who Is Supreme: People, Court or Legislature?" 45 *American Bar Association Journal* 1051–1055 (October, 1959).

Wechsler, Herbert, "Toward Neutral Principles of Constitutional Law," 73 *Harvard Law Review* 1–35 (November, 1959).

Weissman, David L., "The Warren Court and Its Critics," *The Progressive*, May, 1959, pp. 21–24.

Westin, Alan F., "When the Public Judges the Court," *New York Times Magazine*, May 31, 1959, pp. 16ff.

White, J. Patrick, "The Warren Court Under Attack: The Role of the Judiciary in a Democratic Society," 19 *Maryland Law Review* 181–199 (Summer, 1959).

TABLE OF CASES

INDEX

166